SELL THEIR STUFF

BY
T. W. SELLER

THE WHINE SELLER

CONTENTS

ALSO BY T. W. SELLER

http://www.TheWhineSeller.com

NON-FICTION

eBay Marketing Makeover
Beyond Amazon, eBay and Etsy
The Seller Ledger

BY HILLARY DEPIANO

http://www.HillaryDePiano.com

FICTION & PLAYS

The Love of Three Oranges
The Green Bird
The Fourth Orange and other Fairy Tales You've Never
Even Heard Of
The Myrtle
Goosed!
The She-Bear
Arm Candy
Three Padded Walls
Polar Twilight
New Year's Thieve
Daddy Issues
...and more!

INTRODUCTION

I started selling on eBay in 1997 when the site was only a few months old and, in the two decades since then, I've built up my online selling to be my primary source of income. I mention this not to brag but to let you know right from the start that I'm not some random person talking out of my nether regions about something I know nothing about. I've been both a full-time seller and earned a living off of my e-commerce experience not just for a fluke minute but for many years.

And when I tell you that starting a Selling Assistance service isn't just lucrative but easy to do, that's not just talk either because I started my SA business when I was a 17-year-old high school student. If a teenager on dial-up can not only start a business like this but become successful in it, imagine what you could do with your experience and the wealth of superior e-commerce tools available today! While I may have the benefit of experience behind me today, I was once likely even greener than you are right now.

Like most of the early sellers, I didn't start selling online with the intention of making it a business. I started selling partly as a hobby but mostly out of necessity; I had a house full of junk that I wanted to get rid of. Of course, in 1997, online sales were new and e-commerce options few. eBay was one of the only options out there, but even that hadn't yet become the cultural phenomena it is today. Back then, the very idea of selling online was a curiosity, a way to earn a few extra dollars. Now its reputation precedes it, and many sellers approach a site like eBay or Etsy with dollar signs in their eyes, fueled by tales of the riches they can make with the junk in their attic.

Can you make money selling online on a site like eBay? Yes! eBay, Etsy, Craigslist, or the marketplace of your choice can all be fantastic places to earn some extra income and can definitely be built into a full-time business. The evidence of successful sellers using these platforms and others as a full or part-time source of income is everywhere. But it takes work to be a successful seller, and it's not the get-rich-quick scheme some people view it as.

Maybe you're already doing some selling, or maybe you're looking to get started. Veteran or newbie, it all comes down to one thing: where do you get the items to sell? There are dozens of ways to find products. On one end, you sign with a wholesaler, strike deals with suppliers, or manufacture your own products. On the other end, you go to thrift stores and scour discount bins, garage sales, flea markets or even sites like eBay themselves for collectible items to resell. All of these methods are proven ways to make money online, but all of them are a lot of work.

There is an easier way. You can let people who already have a product to sell come to you. You can sell their stuff on consignment and piggyback on their profits in a process known as Selling Assistance.

Unlike starting a traditional retail business, there is no need to contract with wholesalers or purchase tons of inventory you may never sell; you've got complete control over the clients and items you agree to, putting you in charge of your profits. And unlike a traditional store that's locked into regular hours, it's easy to adjust your workload to fit your situation. If you've already established an online business, adding Selling Assistant services is a simple process that can increase your profits.

Acting as a Selling Assistant is one of the most versatile ways of earning income online, and it is easily adaptable to be either full or part time depending on your needs. It's also an ideal work-from-home opportunity, an easy additional income stream for a full-time worker, or an excellent way for stay-at-home parents, students or retirees to make some extra cash. Whether you decide to keep it as supplemental income or build your service up into a full-time business is up to you.

How do I know this? I have successfully served as a Selling Assistant for two decades. I've sold on sites like eBay and Amazon as well as on my own website. I've shifted my Selling Assistant services back and forth between part time and full time to suit my current needs and have adjusted my workload volume to be anywhere from 5% of my income to 90% depending on my current work situation. I can assure you first hand of both the profitability and flexibility of being an SA.

In the chapters that follow, I hope to share with you the wealth of my own experience as a Selling Assistant and to guide you through the process of starting your own consignment business. But before those dollar signs pop back into your eyes, remember, there's going to be work involved. Luckily for you, you've got someone who's been through it all before and knows how to get you started the right way.

Let's do this together…

Sincerely, your Selling Assistant assistant,

T. W. Seller

DISCLAIMER

WHAT IS A SELLING ASSISTANT?
THE ULTIMATE OVERVIEW

WHAT EXACTLY IS A SELLING ASSISTANT?

The term Selling Assistant describes any experienced seller who sells items for other people, usually for a fee or other commission and often on consignment. The fees and terms of this arrangement are determined by the Selling Assistants themselves and can vary widely. You'll also see sellers in this role referred to as Trading Assistants, Listing Assistants, consignment sellers or, if they have a brick and mortar location, Trading Posts or drop-off locations. Throughout this book, I will use the phrase Selling Assistant to refer to anyone selling items for others whether they are working part time out of the home, running a full-time retail storefront, or anywhere in between.

WHAT DOES CONSIGNMENT MEAN?

The terms consignment by itself means either the actual goods being sold or the act of sending something to someone to have it sold. The phrase "on consignment" usually refers to a deal in which a seller only pays for items that sell and may return any unsold items to the original owner. This describes the typical relationship between the SA and the client.

WHAT EXACTLY DOES A SELLING ASSISTANT DO?

Selling Assistants perform all of the tasks associated with selling an item for a client for compensation.

Selling Assistants connect with potential customers either by reaching out to clients themselves or because their marketing drew the clients to them. If the client has items the Selling Assistant is willing to sell, they enter into a contract to do so. Once under a contract, the SA will usually do all of the following for their client's items: clean, research, photograph, write listing text, answer questions during the listing, collect buyer payment upon sale, pack and ship the items, and deal with end-of-sale issues such as returns or other buyer issues. Once the items have sold, the SA subsequently passes any revenue on to the owner less their fee or commission.

I SAID *EXACTLY*. WHAT'S A TYPICAL DAY LIKE?

There is no such thing as a typical day as a Selling Assistant. What your day is *exactly* like is completely up to you and how you've designed your service. That's the beauty of it!

HOW DOES A SELLING ASSISTANT MAKE MONEY?

While every SA can have their own system, most Selling Assistants either take a commission of the final sale price or charge the client a flat fee by item, by hour or by contract.

WHO CAN BECOME A SELLING ASSISTANT?

There are no prerequisites for working as a Selling Assistant. I would recommend that you have at least some prior experience with selling so you know what you're getting into. Anyone who is willing and able to sell items online or off can do so for others, which is one of the things that makes this such a fantastic opportunity. There is nowhere to register, no terms to agree to, no feedback system to cater to, and you'll pay no registration fees for running your service.

Best of all, you can start whenever you're ready without having to wait on anyone else!

WHAT ABOUT EBAY TRADING ASSISTANTS?

eBay used to have the largest and best-known Selling Assistance program. Founded in 2002, any seller in good standing could register as an eBay Trading Assistant (usually individuals working out of their homes), Listing Assistant (eBay Motors), or Trading Post (which later became Registered eBay Drop-Off locations when eBay started to run afoul of local auctioneering laws) and sell items for others on eBay. Some third-party franchises sprang up as Drop-Off locations, and many are still in business to this day. Though eBay shut the program down in 2013 and replaced it with the in-house eBay's Sell For Me Valet service, the eBay Trading Assistant program was really just an unnecessary middleman for what was already a booming business relationship between sellers and those with something to sell.

If you're a former eBay Trading Assistant feeling adrift without the stamp of legitimacy you got from having your service officially registered, I think you'll find that you'll ultimately prefer the freedom of running your services on your own terms. Now you owe no allegiance to any platform, and you don't have to comply to anyone else's terms or contracts, which frees you up to offer customers enticing features eBay would never have allowed like multi-channel selling, email marketing or even external webstores. And while you may miss some of the marketing benefits of being listed in the eBay directory, that was only a single promotional opportunity, and not even a very good one. In the end, getting the freedom to sell your own way without being shackled to the fees and policies of a single platform is well worth the loss of the directory.

WHERE CAN A SELLING ASSISTANT SELL?

While Trading Assistants in eBay's program were limited to selling their clients' items on eBay, the sky's the limit for the independent Selling Assistant. You can tailor your service to just the marketplace that you specialize in or offer multi-channel selling, which is a buzz word that means that you can sell on multiple sites at once to maximize your clients' profits across several platforms. There's a wealth of e-commerce options available these days, and you have the freedom to use whatever best fits you and your clients' needs. Beyond the obvious marketplaces like Amazon, eBay and Etsy, you may also consider selling items through your own webstore, offering local selling through classified ads like Craigslist or even cross listing items both online and in your brick and mortar store.

While I'd recommend starting your service on the marketplace you already have the most experience with and where you feel the most comfortable, it's a great idea to experiment with a variety of selling options. Not only is this an extra selling point for your services because you can give your clients more selection, it's also a good way to future proof your business. Selling on a variety of platforms ensures you won't be screwed over like you would be if your one and only marketplace changes its fees or polices in a way that affects you negatively.

WHAT KIND OF ITEMS CAN A SELLING ASSISTANT SELL?

A Selling Assistant can take on any items that can be legally bought and sold. The items you'll encounter most frequently are home goods, toys and clothing from individuals and families looking for a little extra cash or to free up some space. You'll also find a lot of clients with collectibles and antiques. While most of the items that come your way will fit into these basic categories, there is a wide variety of items clients will offer up for Selling Assistance.

But while a Selling Assistant can sell just about

anything, what you may *choose* to sell is another matter. Selling Assistants can and should refuse items they either don't think are worth their time or that they don't feel comfortable selling. A Selling Assistant that focuses on a specific niche or area of expertise can often have more success than someone who will consign just about anything. However, limiting the type of items you sell can also limit your profit potential. Knowing what items to take on and what to refuse is one of the seemingly small details that can make or break your service.

WHAT IF I'M ALREADY RUNNING A SUCCESSFUL ONLINE BUSINESS?

If you've already established a selling presence, that doesn't mean you need to choose between selling for yourself and selling for others. Combining the two can often do more than just double your business. In fact, the more experienced a seller you are, the more successful you're likely to be as a Selling Assistant. Adding Selling Assistant services to your existing business is a simple way to increase your profits, and it's something any seller should consider offering even as part of a larger company. It's also an excellent way to expand both by the scope of items you sell and by diversifying how you earn your income, giving you an extra protective cushion if things don't go as planned.

Unlike someone for which Selling Assistance is their primary source of income, offering it alongside a healthy selling business makes it easier for you to only take on the clients you're interested in. You've always got a back-up source of income if one part of the company has a slow month. Not to mention that if there's a dead spell without any clients to tempt you, it costs you nothing to just leave your SA option open until something you are interested in comes along.

IS BECOMING A SELLING ASSISTANT RIGHT FOR ME?

Being a Selling Assistant can be very flexible and can easily evolve from a part-time to a full-time source of income.

Because the SA has complete control over her/his own schedule, the job can be adjustable seasonally, is easy to run alongside a full-time job, and is a popular home-based business.

Some people who might want to consider becoming a Selling Assistant:

- Stay-at-home parents

- Students

- Retirees

- Teachers or other seasonal employees

- Someone between full-time jobs or job hunting

- Established online sellers looking for additional income and inventory

- Anyone looking for some extra income or a work-at-home environment

On the other hand, running a business, no matter what kind of business it is, is challenging, and a Selling Assistance business comes with its own host of issues on top of the usual ones. This is not a get-rich-quick scheme, it's just a viable business opportunity that, when done right, can be a good source of income.

There is work aplenty involved in running a successful SA business, but there are also lots of advantages. We'll take a closer look at both throughout this book. Just keep your eyes open and make sure you're thinking realistically as we start to think about the next steps.

HOW DO I GET STARTED AS A SELLING ASSISTANT?

I'm glad you asked! Read on...

DESIGNING YOUR SERVICE

Let's get down to the meat of your SA service. What, exactly, will you be doing for your clients? What will your rates be? What features will you add to attract customers?

One of the best things about starting a Selling Assistance business is how much freedom you have; the options are literally endless, and you have unlimited flexibility in how you run your business. But while all that independence is definitely a good thing, it can be incredibly intimidating, especially when you're first starting out. You could find yourself either paralyzed by the number of decisions you need to make to shape your service or making choices on the fly without considering their consequences.

It's an excellent idea to take the time and make some decisions about your service before you actually start taking on clients. Once you're contracted into your terms, you'll be stuck with them—even if you later realize they weren't a good idea. While you'll likely adjust your policies as you gain experience and your business grows, just a few minutes of planning ahead can save you hundreds of headaches down the road.

To help you narrow down what you might want, this section will run through a variety of aspects to consider. Just keep in mind that what I'm providing here is just a starting point. As you start to shape your service, you'll realize that each decision can spur dozens of others as you consider each angle. When it comes to anything binding like a contract, it's always better to overthink and prepare for any eventuality, no matter how unlikely it seems, than to leave yourself vulnerable.

As we go through each of the sections ahead, do yourself a favor and start jotting down what you decide for each. Here's why: Your list of policies and the contract you'll have buyers sign are both really just a list of what your business will and will not do. If you take the time to record each decision as we go through the options, we'll finish this section and you'll already have the first draft of your contract.

For example, if the next section convinces you to charge a $1 fee per item, write down: "We charge a flat $1 per item fee." *Boom!* You've started your client contract. Painless, right?

MONEY MATTERS

HOW DOES A SELLING ASSISTANT MAKE MONEY?

While there is at least one SA I know of who offers his services entirely for free simply because he thinks selling on eBay is fun, the rest of us would like to see some profit for our hard work. But exactly how your Selling Assistance service makes money is completely up to you, and there is a wide variety of ways to make a profit. From fees to commission, hourly rates to flat charges, or a completely new way that you've dreamed up, these money matters are really the first decision you need to make before you proceed.

Deciding how you'll profit and what you'll charge is only part of the picture. Equally important is having a plan for how you'll handle expenses, such as selling fees or shipping costs, and determining what charges you'll take on as a part of your service and which ones the customer will cover. Lastly, you'll need to come up with a system for keeping track of your sales and earnings and develop a method for paying your clients.

Before you start feeling overwhelmed, let me assure you that it isn't as complicated as it sounds. Let's break it down bit by bit. We'll start with some of the ways you can earn income from your Selling Assistance service.

RESALE

For some clients, it might make sense for you to just buy all of their items outright and then make your profit when you resell them for more than you paid. In other words, you'd pay them a flat amount upfront for everything and then you'd sell the items yourself, keeping all the income. Flipping items like this, to borrow a phrase from the real estate market where you buy something specifically to resell it for a profit, can be risky but also profitable if done correctly.

This way is certainly simpler than any other option, as

the client gets a check when you pick up the items and they aren't involved with the selling or shipping elements at all. There's no need to charge a fee or commission because you'll make your profits on the resale. If your client is in a rush (for instance they sold their house and need everything gone before the closing or is in some financial trouble and need money to pay off some debts) and is more concerned with having the items gone quickly or getting money fast, this is an excellent solution.

There can be a few disadvantages to this. The first and most obvious is that this isn't really what either you or the client signed up for, as it's not a consignment arrangement. You wouldn't be helping them sell their items, so it's not actually Selling Assistance at all. It puts the owner of the items into the role of a wholesaler or dealer rather than a SA client. It would also involve a completely different contract from your SA services.

Secondly, you would need to make sure you buy the items from the client at a low enough price that you'll be able to make enough of a profit on the resale to make it worth your time, which can be a challenge. What value would be high enough to satisfy the client but still leave meat enough on the bone for you? For that matter, what value could you offer that would be fair to the client so they won't feel cheated? That's going to be a hard number to find unless you're incredibly familiar with the type of items you're being offered. More traditional ways of monetizing your SA service, such as fees and commissions, are surer things when it comes to making a profit.

Why am I starting this section with an option that isn't really Selling Assistance at all? As soon as you start to advertise that you're willing to get people cash for their stuff, all sorts will start contacting you with items. In addition to the ones who understand and want your SA consignment services as designed, you're going to get clients who just want to sell you their items upfront without bothering with the SA element. In addition to the examples I gave above of the client that's in a rush or in need of fast cash, you'll also have clients that don't really understand what your service is. They may find the whole concept of Selling Assistance too confusing and would prefer to just sell the items to you directly. While you'll usually want to steer these clients towards your prepackaged SA services, where you're more likely to make the best profit, sometimes the resale route might be the better choice for either you or the client.

In short, don't ever discount the possibility entirely. There will be times you think you're going into a typical Selling Assistance relationship when it suddenly becomes items for sale that you could resell, and you should have a plan in place for that eventuality. Staying flexible is one of the secrets to running a successful business, and this service is no exception.

FEES

For our purposes, a fee is a flat charge. You may choose to charge a fee per item, per hour, per client, per month or on a scale based on various factors. Fees charged can also depend on whether the item sells, on the type of item, how much the item sells for, or other factors. Even SAs that work on commission charge fees in some cases.

Here are a few examples of ways to earn your SA income through fees:

- Per item fees can be a simple flat fee that you charge per listing or a tiered pricing structure based on what the item ultimately sells for. You can also determine a per item fee by type of item, ensuring that you'll always earn more on something that you know is difficult or otherwise takes more time to list.

- Fees can be used as insurance to make sure you profit no matter the circumstance. You could charge a fee on items that do not sell, an additional fee for particularly challenging items, or even a storage fee for keeping client items in your home or office.

- Fees can also be adapted to an hourly pay rate where the SA would bill the client at the end of the job based on how long it took. This method ensures that your payment is guaranteed no matter how the listings ultimately do.

- Similarly, you can charge a single flat fee per client. You name a single price to sell all of their items for them and they pay only that, regardless of what ensues in between.

Advantages to Fees

- Fees can ensure that you make money regardless of whether the items sell or not, letting you take more risks with the kinds of clients you take on.

- Fees guarantee you a certain profit threshold even when the item's final sale price is low.

- Compared to commission, they provide a steady and easy to predict income.

- A flat fee for the job or hourly fee can mean higher profits than tying your fate to the final sale price of your items.

Disadvantages to Fees

- Fees can be a client turn-off. Even the word "fee" itself is loaded and, psychologically, it's often thought of as a penalty. Clients may balk at the flat costs or suffer from sticker shock seeing everything totaled in front of them when they'd likely be perfectly happy to pay more than that if the costs were spread out as lots of small commissions.

- Setting realistic and profitable fee prices can be difficult, especially when starting out. It's very easy to underestimate how much to charge, but high fees will immediately scare clients away.

- Your profit remains the same no matter what you're selling or how it sells. For instance, you might make the same $5 per item fee on a Barbie outfit that sold for $1.50 as you do on the designer luggage set that sold for

$4,000.

The key to fees is predictability. It's the assurance that you'll always make something for your work. It's just making sure that what you make is worth the money and that your rates are something the client will agree to, and that's the real challenge.

COMMISSIONS

Just like a salesperson in a retail store, the SA that works on commission makes profit on a percentage basis based on how the items sell. For instance, the SA could take a percentage of the final sale price of each item, the sale price of the item less selling fees, or a percentage of the total profit made by the owner of the items.

Clients often prefer commission for reasons that are mostly psychological, but it provides some challenges for the SA.

Advantages of working on commission

- Commission increases the level of trust between the SA and the client. The client knows that the SA will do everything in their power to get the maximum profit on their items because the amount the SA herself makes is dependent on the final value. Commission means the SA's profit is directly proportionate to the sort of job she or he does (i.e., the more you sell it for, the more you make), and that gives a potential client more confidence in your service. It's in both parties' best interests to get the best price possible, and that gives the transaction a collaborative feeling of working together.

- A commission makes your service seem less expensive, even if it isn't really. Even though a commission can often mean the client pays more in the end, a flat fee can sound higher because you're giving them an exact total instead of talking about a percentage of a future number. It's a mind game, but it works.

- The SA makes more on high-selling items than with fees.

Remember that $4,000 designer luggage? Unless you're charging a 0.1% commission, you're guaranteed to be making more than $5 on that item.

Disadvantages of working on commission

- Profit becomes difficult to predict and can vary widely from item to item. You'll take a gamble with every new client you take. Will their items sell for enough to be worth the work of listing them?

- Commission can corner the SA into a poor work-to-financial-return ratio on items that sell for very little. You spent 40 hours listing all those LPs, and they only sold for $10 total? No matter what your commission rate is, you made less than pennies per hour for your work. There are ways to avoid this situation, but you can still find yourself in it no matter how prepared you are.

- The SA makes no commission on items that do not sell.

Commission is a bit like betting the success of your business entirely on your selling skills and your ability to pick the right items. It can be an unreliable form of profit but, like the stock market, if you play it right, it can mean much greater profits than flat fee. Is a little unpredictability worth the chance of making more money?

A COMBINATION OF FEES AND COMMISSION

Still not sure which option is best? Many SAs use a combination of fees and commissions. For example, a SA might charge a commission that is a percentage of the final sale price of items that sold, and then charge a flat fee on items that did not sell.

You might also create two different pricing structures and let your clients take their pick. Just make sure that both work out favorably for you in the end. A business has to make money after all, and you don't want to sell yourself short.

Once you've weighed all the options, take the elements

you like from each and start to craft your personal profit plans.

WHAT DO YOU DO?

You're probably wondering what profit method I use in my SA service, and I'm happy to tell you. However, understand that I'm not telling you to sway you one way or the other but rather because it feels dishonest not to be upfront about exactly what I do, especially since you were likely curious. Your experiences with either fees or commissions may be totally different to mine, so please don't take this as my recommendation that you go one way or another, that is still entirely up to you.

I exclusively charge a commission of 20% on the final sale price of items I sell for SA clients. I know this rate is lower than average—I've seen many who charge 35% or more—but I'm careful about what clients I take on, and 20% works for me. I used to charge a $1 per item in addition to the commission, but clients routinely complained about it, so I dropped it. That extra $1 an item wasn't worth losing customers over.

The main appeal of a commission to me has always been the trust factor. A client is less likely to argue with me if an item sold for less than they'd hoped for because they understand that I had as much at stake in it selling for more as they did. Obviously, I would have gotten a higher price if it had been possible to increase my own profit. It changes the SA-to-client relationship to more of a partnership where we are in it together, our destinies tied to the same final sale price. But I can tell you from personal experience, it's very easy to get burned when items that were a lot of work to list don't sell for much. Research, realism and knowing when to say no to items are your best defense against this.

DEPOSITS

A deposit isn't a way to profit, but it's still part of your most basic financial terms. Not all SAs use a deposit, but it's something to consider. There are two main types of deposits.

SA TO CLIENT DEPOSIT

Many clients feel more secure if you have given them a security deposit, which will end up being an advance on their profit once you've sold the items. In the case of very expensive or fragile items, this can make the client feel better about a complete stranger driving off with their items. For most items, however, a contract ensuring compensation for lost or damaged items can stand in the place of a SA to Client Deposit. Should you decide to give your client a deposit, however, make sure there is a solid paper trail of the process with the terms clearly outlined in the event of trouble later on. You'll want to make sure you get that advance back if their items never sell, which is why I would only recommend this when dealing with items you are 100% certain will be successful.

CLIENT TO SA DEPOSIT

It is not uncommon for a SA to ask a client for a deposit to cover the initial listing fees for their items. They'll get this money back when you send them their first payment. While some clients will balk at this, it is a helpful security measure for the SA, particularly when dealing with a new client. The purpose of this deposit is to cover eBay and PayPal fees for the initial batch of listings before the items sell and you've received payment. It's particularly useful when dealing with items that you either suspect will not sell well (or at all) or for clients that have done a bait and switch (promised you treasures and then sent over entirely different, and worthless, items).

A client once contracted me to sell a collection of vintage dolls. Once we'd solidified the deal, she mailed me a box, but instead of being filled with the dolls, it was full of old sweaters I knew would never sell with a note that she'd changed her mind and I was to sell these instead. I couldn't get a reply despite repeated phone calls, emails and finally a printed letter. Foolishly (this was back when I was a teenager and just starting out), I tried to sell the sweaters in the hopes that then she'd give me the promised dolls. After trying twice to sell the sweaters, I not only hadn't sold any of them, but I was now out two week's worth of eBay fees with no way of being compensated for them. I ended up donating the sweaters to charity after months of no contact and eating the eBay fees.

It was after this incident that I started to require a $25 deposit from new clients. The first week of listings with a new client, I list just enough so that their deposit will cover all fees and then proceed with listing everything else once I know that their items are sellable. Honestly, I've had to waive the deposit many times for clients that balked at it. Oddly enough, every client that balked at the Client to SA Deposit requested a SA to Client Deposit instead. It can seem like backwards logic to you since you're the one who's going to have to front the cash for their potentially worthless items but, to the client, they're giving you amazing treasures and they want some financial protection.

DISTRIBUTING SELLING FEES AND SHIPPING EXPENSES

Once you have an idea of how you'll profit from your service, you'll want to take into account the fees and other costs associated with selling the item. Will your business take on all of these costs or will some of these be passed on to the buyers? It's not as simple a question as it first seems.

Every cost your business covers is an additional feature to attract clients to your service but also another expense that leeches from your bottom line. You're already profiting from the sale of their items by the fees or commission you charge—should that cover any additional costs? Which costs seem appropriate to expect the client to pay and when are you just being greedy?

While you could conceivably ask your clients to pay a

portion of any of your business expenses, there are a few that are the most common.

WHO PAYS THE SELLING AND PAYMENT PROCESSING FEES ON THE SALE?

No matter where you sell, most marketplaces and platforms charge fees per sale, and you'll be paying those fees on your clients' items. In the same way, every time you sell anything, you'll end up paying your credit card processor transaction fees on that payment. While these fees are usually small, they can add up, especially as your sales volume increases.

Let's say you just sold a client's item on eBay. As far as eBay is concerned, that transaction is no different from any other one you'd do on the site. The fees are billed to the seller's eBay account as usual regardless of whether it's an SA item or not and you'll need to pay eBay for them. PayPal will also take their fees out of each payment you receive for those items. You may also have additional selling fees such as listing upgrades, picture hosting fees, or other third-party services.

Many SAs opt to bill their clients for selling and payment processing fees. The simplest way to do this is to just subtract these fees out of the client's profits before you send them their payment. You'll want to make sure your documentation and contract makes it crystal clear that this is what you'll be doing upfront so they don't feel cheated when they get their check.

There are a few other things to consider. Since they'll be paying the fees on them, will you let clients opt out of listing upgrades or other additional fees? Will you be passing any discounts or promotional listing rates on to your clients or will they always pay the posted rates regardless of what you actually paid? Whatever you decide, just make sure you spell it out in your contract to avoid confusion and unhappiness later.

I've always passed all actual selling and payment processing fees on to my clients, though I present it as a feature.

Because I'm a volume seller and storeowner, I get discounts on fees and more free listings per month than they would get on their own, and so I spin this as additional value I can offer them over selling their items themselves. Since they'd be incurring these fees anyway if they sold their items themselves, I've never had anyone complain about having to cover the selling fees, especially since they are so small.

That said, I sell on commission, and a low commission at that. If you're charging a higher commission or a flat fee, your clients may expect you to cover those fees from your profits. It's up to you to draw that line where it's worth it to eliminate that expense from your profits, and when it's worth it to shoulder those costs to attract more clients.

WHO PAYS THE SHIPPING COSTS?

There are several scenarios when it comes to shipping, but no matter how you're shipping your items, someone's got to pay for the shipping. Will it be you or your client? Or is there a third option?

Most of us are already charging our buyers directly for the shipping costs when they purchase something from us. As long as what the buyer pays covers everything, and that's usually the case when you're talking about calculated shipping using the actual item weights, couldn't we just leave shipping out of the SA equation entirely since the buyer has already paid it? Or course, if you did still bill the client for those shipping costs, you could turn that into a source of profit instead of a breakeven point.

If your shipping costs don't cover the cost of shipping or if they only cover it some of the time, it might make sense to have your client shoulder some of that burden. If you offer free shipping on all your items—free shipping can be very attractive for buyers, thus increasing your sales—shouldering these costs yourself can eat up your profits very quickly, so you may want to bill the client for them. But shipping costs, especially international costs or overnight, can be very high and your clients may not like the sticker shock.

If you're charging a flat-rate shipping cost and you lose money on some shipments, you may also want your clients to cover all or some of this burden. But would you charge the clients for the actual shipping or the flat rate the buyer paid? The whole shipping costs or just the difference between actual and charged shipping? Would you pass the loss from each shipment on to them directly? Would you do the same if there was a profit?

If you do decide to pass shipping charges, either whole or in part, on to your clients, there are a few more things to consider.

- If you charge a handling fee in addition to the shipping costs, would you pass that on to the client?

- Where do shipping upgrades such as insurance, signature or delivery confirmation fit in? Will you require the client to pay for protection like insurance on certain items such as fragile or delicate items?

- What happens when an item is returned? Will your client have to shoulder return shipping costs?

OTHER COSTS TO CONSIDER

While shipping and selling costs may seem obvious, there's a host of other expenses that can arise over the course of a Selling Assistance job. You'll want to take the time to consider these options in advance so you can protect yourself against them in your contracts and agreements. Always make sure your clients understand the nature of any incidentals to avoid unpleasant surprises. Worst case, if a charge that you feel the client will have to be responsible for arises after the contract is signed, you can ask them to sign an addendum outlining the new charges. However, as they won't always agree to such a change, you'll want to cover yourself ahead of time wherever possible or you'll end up footing the bill.

If any of the following are deemed needed or requested

by either party, will you or your client be responsible for the cost of…

- Repairs or restorations?

- Appraisals or consultations with a specialist?

- Additional storage for unwieldy or awkward items, a large quantity of items or items with unusual needs?

- Vehicle rental for items that neither the client's nor SA's car can transport?

- Packing supplies if the client's item involves unique or unusual shipping or handling requirements?

Those are just a few examples of the kind of surprise costs a client's items could incur, and nearly all of them could be a nasty twist if you haven't budgeted for them or made an agreement as to who will be responsible.

HOW DOES THE CLIENT MAKE MONEY?

There are really two main ways your client makes money from your service. If you're just buying your client's items outright to resell, you've already paid your client that flat rate, so that's already taken care of. If you're charging a fee or commission, however, you'll most likely be paying your client the actual value their items sold for less any expenses.

Just as you were probably most focused on how you'd earn money from your service, this is the aspect that your client is the most concerned with. Otherwise reasonable people tend to become much more paranoid, impatient, and… well… crazed when money is involved. It's your responsibility to make sure that you handle all these money issues professionally and in strict accordance with the terms you outlined upfront to give your clients confidence in your abilities and trust that you won't swindle them.

HOW DO I KNOW HOW MUCH TO PAY MY CLIENT?

Saying that you'll pay your client the actual value their items sold for is really an oversimplification because, depending on how you decided to handle your SA fees and/or commission, shipping and selling fees or other expenses, there are several deductions you'll need to make from that number before you actually send a payment. Of all the elements of your business, this is the one you want to be the most careful with. Mistakes can lead anywhere from a lawsuit from a client you shortchanged to you overpaying, and those extra dollars will not be easy to get back, if ever.

While your equation will vary slightly depending on how you're allocating everything, here's the basic breakdown:

[AMOUNT ITEM SOLD FOR] - [SELLING & PAYMENT PROCESSING FEES] - [SA FEE OR COMMISSION] - [ANY ADDITIONAL CHARGES]
= [AMOUNT DUE CLIENT]

Let's do a quick example. Let's say I'm your SA and your item sold on eBay for $1,000. The eBay and PayPal fees I'm holding you responsible for total $130.59, and I charge a 35% commission on the final sale price, which comes to $350. I didn't bill you for anything else, so it's a simple matter of punching our values into the equation above.

$1000 - $130.59 - $350 = $519.41

I owe you $519.41.

Did you look at that number and think, dang, I didn't get much of that fictional $1,000? Now you've got a sense of what it's like to be a Selling Assistance client and why it's important to make sure your client is informed ahead of time about the various costs and deductions. But remember, presentation is everything. How you present the payment to your client and report all the expenses will be a big factor in how they react to the bottom line. Deductions look much more drastic when looking at an individual transaction than when applied to the total of the whole contract.

HOW DO I PAY MY CLIENT?

There is a wide variety of ways to send payments these days, but it's hard to find a simpler option than a good old bank check. If you do decide to issue client payment via check, however, you should really consider opening a checking account specifically for your business. Many banks have a free business checking option, so this shouldn't be an extra expense, and it will make your business look that much more professional than if you're using your personal checks.

In most cases, there are no charges or transaction fees on a check. There are some expenses involved with this method of payment, however, namely the cost of the printed check itself and the postage it takes to mail it to the client. If your bank offers free bill pay with your checking account, that's a simple way to avoid both of these costs. With bill pay, your bank will issue, print and mail the check for you for no additional charge, so there's no need to purchase paper checks or stamps to mail them.

If checks aren't an option, you may want to consider PayPal. PayPal is fast, and the money from the sale of the client's items may already be in your account. PayPal does charge a transaction fee on every payment transfer that you can either pay yourself or pass on for the client to pay. If you don't keep a balance in your PayPal account, you can also use them to process eChecks.

That said, not everyone has a PayPal account, and you can't exactly force your client to open one to claim their payment. This is an issue with most electronic forms of payment; while it's common for sellers like us to have accounts at these services, regular people seldom do. While it can seem like the obvious solution to you, it may not be a practical solution for your client.

Another option is to pay via money order. Money orders are easy to get and are sold everywhere from your local post office to Walmart. That said, most money orders have a maximum value they can be issued for, must be purchased in cash, and can cost anywhere from one to several dollars to purchase. You'll also still have to delivery or ship them to your buyer, which would require the cost of a stamp. Wire transfers, bank drafts, MoneyGrams etc. are also all fast, but the costs can eat into your profits.

No matter what method of payment you choose, make sure there is a paper trail so you can prove that you paid your client as promised. There's no way to prove that your client received your payment if you paid them via money order or cash. A canceled check or transaction record from a site like PayPal, Western Union, or MoneyGram all show that your buyer received their payment, and that's much better than just having your word against theirs.

WHAT KIND OF REPORTING SHOULD I INCLUDE WITH MY CLIENT'S PAYMENT?

Before you send any kind of payment, you'll want to give your clients a breakdown of everything related to their contract with you. How you draw up this reconciliation is up to you, but I think it's better to err on the side of complete transparency when it comes to money (both what they owe and what you owe them) even if it means a lot of documentation. As long as you put the most important parts right up top where the client can easily find them, they can, and often will, skip the rest. So, while you technically could just give the client a single line with the total amount their items sold for, total fees, your total commission and what they are owed, it's better to give them a list of each transaction individually so they can see exactly where the money went.

I used to spend hours on my client sheets, transferring each fee into neat little rows in a spreadsheet so clients could see the whole story of each item in fees and profits at a glance, but I finally realized that clients weren't reading these details at all and were only focusing on the totals on the top unless they wanted to look up a specific item. I was wasting my time. Now, I just take my actual selling invoices, copy out only the transactions related to each SA client and just put those line items directly into a spreadsheet. I add the PayPal fees in manually, though you could likely do this in bulk as well by downloading your payment processing history and copying those entries over the same way. If I'm utilizing multiple marketplaces for this contract, the only other thing I'll do is add a column to indicate which site each transaction was from, but I don't bother if everything was sold on the same platform.

You may decide, for the sake of time, to add a clause to your agreement with your client stating that you will charge standard or posted selling and payment processing fees on each item. If you're savvy with your spreadsheet program, you can write a formula to automatically calculate those fees for you, saving time. Instead of looking up each individual transaction, you'll just bill the client the standard posted fees associated with a listing like theirs. But while this is a timesaver, you can often shortchange yourself because the standard rate may not take into account cross-border rates or other fees. It can also often result in overcharging your client. If, for example, a single buyer bought three of your client's items and only made one payment for all three, you'd be triple-charging your client for the PayPal fees on that one item by only using posted fees.

Let me show you a small section of a reconciliation sheet I did for a SA client I sold some items for on eBay as an example:

				Fee Total	Payment Cleared	Paypal Fees	TA Fee	Total Due Owner
			Totals	$133.65	$1,255.59	$53.69	$251.12	$817.13
Date	Item Name	Item number	Type of fee	Fee Amount	Payment Cleared	Paypal Fees		
Jun-02-13 18:29:21 PDT			Buy It Now Listing Fee	$ 0.25				
Jun-02-13 18:29:21 PDT			Insertion Fee;Promotional Rate	$ 0.25				
May-05-13 12:39:18 PDT			Insertion Fee;Promotional Rate	$ 0.20				
Jun-09-13 18:29:23 PDT			Final Value Fee	$ 6.03	$ 67.00	$ 2.46		
Jun-10-13 11:12:24 PDT			Final Value Fee on Shipping	$ 0.69				
Jun-02-13 18:29:22 PDT			Buy It Now Listing Fee	$ 0.25				
Jun-02-13 18:29:22 PDT			Insertion Fee;Promotional Rate	$ 0.25				
Jun-02-13 18:29:27 PDT			International Site Visibility Fee	$ 0.10				
May-12-13 17:38:32 PDT			Insertion Fee;Promotional Rate	$ 0.20				
May-12-13 17:38:35 PDT			International Site Visibility Fee	$ 0.50				
Jun-09-13 18:29:24 PDT			Final Value Fee	$ 8.82	$ 98.00	$ 5.65		

I've blurred the item numbers and titles, but the rest are the real fees and final sale prices I copied over directly from my eBay invoice. EBay invoices download in your choice of either

HTML or CSV. I choose CSV because they open easily in any spreadsheet program such as Microsoft Office Excel or free options like Google Sheets. Once in a spreadsheet, you can use simple formulas to do any calculations for you.

Next I add a few columns at the top.

- **Total Fees** is just a total of the column with all the selling fees.

- **Payment Cleared** is the total of the column where I manually input each item's Final Sale Price once it's cleared. This info already appears on the invoice, but it's part of the Final Value Fee line, so you'll need to retype it into its own cell if you want to be able to tally it using a formula. We'll get more into how I determine a payment to be cleared in the next section.

- **PayPal Fees** is the total of the column where I input the PayPal fees. I input them on the same line as the Final Sale Price to make it easier for the client to follow.

- **SA Commission** is a formula cell that calculates my commission so it automatically updates as items sell. I charged this client a 20% commission, so that cell is showing 20% of Payment Cleared.

- **Total Due Owner** is another formula showing what I owe the client. It's actually [PAYMENT CLEARED] - [TOTAL FEES] - [PAYPAL FEES] - [SA COMMISSION].

The Payment Cleared column will usually match the Final Value column. However, in the case of a non-paying bidder, return, or a partial refund, the amount the buyer pays may end up being different to what was expected, and this allows you to reflect this. Also, in the case of non-paying bidder items, this allows you to place zero in that column to denote that the sale wasn't completed.

At the bottom of the sheet, I document any payments made. I list the payment dollar values, their check numbers, the dates the payments were issued and the balance of what I still owe the client. While clients with only a few items may get everything in a single payment, a client with many items or an extended contract may get multiple payments before we complete our dealings.

Though not reflected in my screenshot, I use a little color-coding to make a few things stand out, especially when sending out a partial payment. I put a key at the bottom of the spreadsheet and color certain rows to denote things such as sales that are still ongoing, items that were returned, or items that have been paid for but the payment hasn't cleared. Even these minor extra steps only take a few minutes, and I'm able to give my clients a detailed reckoning that looks like it took hours though it really only took a few minutes.

If you're charging the client for things I'm not, such as shipping costs or other fees, or if you're not holding the client responsible for selling or payment fees, you'll need to adjust accordingly.

I present my sheets sorted by item title then item number, which is why the dates jump around the way they do in the example above. But sorting it this way instead of by date, which is how they come from eBay, it more clearly tells the story of each item fee by fee. It also makes it easier for the client to see where all the numbers come from.

No matter how you decide to do your reporting, keep in mind three things:

1. It should be simple and fast to do so you aren't wasting your valuable time on something the client may never even glance at.

2. It should be thorough just in case there's a problem later so you have proof that you gave your client a complete record of all transactions and there's a paper trail to protect you.

3. And, lastly, it should be easy and preferably free to send to the client.

I usually just email my spreadsheet to the client directly as soon as I'm finished so I don't have to pay for postage, but if you're already sending a snail-mail payment, keep it light enough that you can include it in the same envelope without an additional postage cost. Google Sheets even has a simple sharing option that lets you share the live spreadsheet with the client directly instead of sending them a static copy.

WHEN SHOULD I PAY MY CLIENT?

Let's say your client's item sells right now, should you immediately send them the payment for it? Not so fast! A transaction isn't finished when a buyer pays for the item. In some ways, it's only just beginning.

Once an item sells, you'll often get the payment at the same time, but not always. Depending on your payment terms, the buyer may have anywhere from days to a couple of weeks to pay for the item after committing to buy. If you don't get payment, you'll need to go through the non-paying bidder process before you can relist it, and that takes time. Even if the buyer does pay right away, they may pay via a method like eCheck, which takes a week to clear.

Either way, you'll wait to ship the item until you get a cleared payment. Then shipping takes time—anywhere from a day to two months for some international shipments. But if the package is delayed or, worse yet, lost in transit, you're looking at more delays even if it does eventually arrive.

Once the item arrives at the buyer's door, that may be the end of the transaction, or it may arrive damaged, and you'll need to go through the insurance claims process. It's possible the buyer will want to return it, which can cause yet more delays as you wait for them to ship it back, and then you'll have to start the timer all over again when you relist it.

The takeaway here is that until you've been paid for the item, the buyer has it in their hands and is satisfied with it, the transaction isn't truly over. If you'd paid your client the moment the listing ended, there are hundreds of things that could have gone wrong with the transaction in the ensuing weeks. You have to build time into the payment window you promise your clients to protect yourself from things that can and will go wrong.

But how much time? It depends on a variety of factors including how long your window for returns is and whether you sell internationally. If you accept returns for up to 30 days after item receipt, you shouldn't promise your clients a payment sooner than 60 or more days from the date of sale to build in time for shipping, slow payments, or other issues. Of course, this time frame is the worst-case scenario, and you'll often be able to pay your clients much sooner. But it's always better to under-promise and over-deliver, and you'll need to leave yourself that extra time just in case.

In my SA business, I've invented some verbiage to explain this payment delay to clients that you may be able to adapt to your business. After explaining that marketplaces like eBay and Amazon require returns and that we've got to build in time for both those and shipping times, I explain that PayPal can reverse a payment for up to 60 days after receipt. Therefore, I don't consider a payment to have "cleared" until that period has elapsed and the transaction becomes permanent and can no longer be reversed. However, if a buyer leaves positive feedback about the item they bought or emails me to say how pleased they are with their purchase, then it's safe to assume that they won't be returning it. In that case, I'll consider that transaction complete and that payment cleared early even though the normal time period isn't up.

Keep in mind that the 60 days I just mentioned only applies from the moment you receive payment. You'll also need to build in time to clean, photograph and list the items for sale as well as for the sale period itself. Auctions may only take a week, but a fixed-price item could sit for months before it sells. It takes some finesse to manage client expectations because people tend to think of selling online as very fast when, in reality, it's surprisingly slow.

If your client only has a few items, you'll probably want to pay them for all of them in a single payment. If there are a large number of items or if some of their items are taking a long time to sell or otherwise clear, you may want to send them a partial payment at different points in the contract. I've had clients that keep giving me new items, so their relationship with me ends up lasting years. Their reconciliation report ends up being several pages long, and I just send them a payment every few months or so until everything is gone.

The danger to partial payments is that you've got to protect yourself and make sure to never overpay your clients. Unless it's impossible, my personal safeguard is to always make sure I've at least listed all the client's items before I send them a single payment. This way I've already taken into account all listing and upgrade fees so that, even if nothing else ever sells from this client after I send that payment, I won't be out those fees.

When I do partial payments, I include all fees on the sheet but only add the sale prices in for items I consider to have cleared, either by passing my 60-day window or because the buyer left feedback or contacted me about the item in a favorable manner. This is great from a client's standpoint because payments usually get larger as we go since the bulk of the fees came off that first payment. Then, as additional sales come in or the client gives me additional items to sell, I just add them to the same sheet, making sure to take past payments into account before making any new ones. Sometimes this means a client gives me their items and gets their final payment within days, and sometimes they have to wait months or even years before we're finally completely done. But I've found that as long as you have good communication, are upfront with exactly what is going on and transparent about everything, and make partial payments whenever possible, clients are understanding about the delay.

But not everyone will be. Some people are looking for fast cash, and they'll balk when they see your payment window. You'll need to decide whether it's better to risk making that time cushion smaller or try to convince those reluctant clients to either trust that it hopefully won't take as long as you advertise or to just sell you their items outright.

MONEY MATTERS MANAGED

If you took notes during that last section, you should have a rough draft of all the financial details of your Selling Assistance service sketched out. As these are the most important terms of your business, it's worth taking a moment to double-check them. Have you made a decision on all of the following?

- How will you profit from your selling services?

  o   Are you open to just purchasing your clients' items outright and reselling them?

  o   Will you charge a fee or commission? What will it be?

  o   Will you require or offer a deposit?

- What selling costs will the SA pass on to the client?

  o   Will the client be responsible for selling fees or payment processing costs?

  o   Will you bill the client all or in part for the cost of packaging or shipping?

  o   Will the client pay actual fees or posted costs for each item?

  o   What other fees should your client expect to cover?

- What expectations should the client have about receiving their payments?

  o   What methods of payment will you offer?

  o   What kind of records and reporting will you offer the client at the end of their contract?

  o   How long after giving you their items should they expect payment?

YOUR SELLING SITUATION

WHERE AND HOW SHOULD I SELL?

Well, where are you selling now? Because the marketplaces you're already the most experienced with are your best bets for selling client items. You don't want to be learning a whole new selling system while you're trying to start up a new service.

Of course, as you grow into your SA service, you'll want to experiment with how you sell so you'll always be able to choose the right platform for the situation. Stay flexible and open to selling on a variety of platforms. If you're selling for a crafter, you'll probably want to list on Etsy. For a client with a lot of media, Amazon or Half.com might be the better fit. You may have the most success selling on Craigslist for that client with large or difficult-to-ship items.

Some things to consider when choosing a marketplace are:

- **how well the marketplace fits the items you have to sell,** which will determine how well and how fast they sell

- **the cost of selling there,** such as fees and other expenses

- **policies and restrictions** that could affect your business

- **Tools, features and upgrades** that make your job easier

- **speed of the sale**

If I'm selling an item for myself, I can afford to be patient; I can let that item linger in my own webstore for weeks until the right buyer comes along with the best price. That's not always the case with Selling Assistant items. You'll want a marketplace where you cannot only be sure that the item will sell but also that it will sell quickly, even if that means taking a slightly lower price than your ideal.

If you're not selling anywhere yet and don't know where to start, look for the venue that best fits the kind of items you'll be specializing in. But then, all things being equal, sell where you're the most comfortable. If your selling skills lie with a particular marketplace, that can make up for all sorts of deficiencies in the platform itself.

MULTI-CHANNEL CONSIGNMENT SELLING

The healthiest business is never completely reliant on any one service or tool, which is why you'll always want to be selling client items on a variety of platforms. There are many advantages of selling through multiple channels, from having increased exposure for your items to diversifying your selling so you'll never be so dependent on a single marketplace that you'll live and die by its changes. Multi-channel selling can mean spreading a client's items out across several platforms or double listing the same items in multiple locations simultaneously to reach several types of buyer at once.

Of course, selling across multiple sites means more to keep track of and more potential to mess things up. You'll need to be very organized to pull it off, keeping sales and sites separate while still keeping track of which items belong to which client contract. But when you free yourself from the idea that you can only sell on a single platform, you'll open yourself up to a variety of selling opportunities.

Having good inventory synchronization, preferably automated, is key. The same items listed on multiple sites is a great way to expand the item's reach and get it in front of as many potential buyers as possible. But what happens if you forget to delist and accidentally sell it twice? Trying to keep your inventory synchronized manually is challenging enough on a single platform, and the problem increases exponentially with additional sites in the mix. Luckily, there are a variety of third-party tools that offer automated synchronization between the most popular selling sites so that when your client's book sells on Amazon, it's automatically marked out of stock on both eBay and your webstore. Automated inventory management is an additional expense, but the cross-promotional benefits to your client's items may make it worth it.

Reporting for a contract where items were sold on

multiple sites can also be a challenge. You may need to consolidate fees from multiple invoices on a single reconciliation spreadsheet, and that data entry can be time-consuming. Personally, I just copy the relevant lines exactly from the selling invoices from each site and paste them directly onto the spreadsheet I give my client. Not only does this allow me to use the spreadsheet itself to calculate the fees and totals, it shows the client exactly what I received from the platform, keeping things completely transparent. Add a column simply to indicate which site each transaction refers to and you're done.

GETTING SELLING ASSISTANCE PRACTICE BEFORE YOU START TAKING ON CLIENTS

If you aren't selling anywhere yet or have only limited experience, you should really get some practice selling before you begin. Clients are trusting you with their items and potential profits because you're presenting yourself as an experienced seller. If you're really just starting out yourself, you're going to be making mistakes that could damage your reputation before you even get started! Even if you're a veteran seller, selling items for someone else can be very different from selling your own items, and you want to make sure you understand what you're in for before you dive in.

A simple way to practice at being a SA before actually starting your service is to buy a large, mixed lot of items of the type you'd like to sell with your service either at a garage sale or on a site like eBay. Let's say that I'm interested in specializing in action figures, but I want some more selling practice before I jump into taking on clients. I find a mixed lot of over 100 random action figures on eBay, and I buy it somewhat blind. Then I proceed to go through the lot I purchased as if it were from a client, organizing, cleaning, researching, photographing and listing each item the way that will yield the most profit. Actually going through this process will give you an idea of the questions you'll need to be asking yourself on each contract ("Would the Avengers figures sell for more if I list them each individually or should I list them as a lot because that's faster?"), and what kind of things you should see if the client can answer to save you time ("Which weapons go with which figure?").

Keep careful track of how long the entire process takes. Once all the items have sold, make up an itemized spreadsheet of all the fees and profits as if you were giving it to a client as a receipt. You may not make a profit on this practice lot, but that's OK, as it's a business expense and a worthwhile investment to get a feel for the SA life in a practice environment. It's well worth a little loss to get some hands-on experience to help you anticipate issues and get a sense of how long different steps in the process are going to take.

Just a word of warning. You'll get better at this as you go. Your first time selling someone else's items will take much longer than it will in the future. You'll need to do less research with each item you list, the work will go faster as you develop a system and, most importantly, you'll develop the sense to only take on items that will be worth it to list, something that may not be the case with your lot of practice items. So, while practice is a good idea, don't assume you'd be a terrible SA if your practice goes poorly.

DO YOU NEED A STOREFRONT OR STANDALONE WEBSTORE?

You don't need your own webstore to offer Selling Assistance services, but you may want one anyway. If you already have a thriving webstore, great! That's just another selling option to offer your clients. But if you don't and you're wondering if now's the time to get one, I'd advise waiting.

Run your SA service for a while out of a marketplace environment such as eBay or Etsy. Then, if you later decide to upgrade, you'll have a better sense of what your needs are from a webstore so you won't go into the process naive. You may even discover that a marketplace is a better platform for your needs anyway, and then you can just save yourself the money and trouble of setting up a standalone webstore.

Many marketplaces also give you a storefront for free as

part of your account, though some, such as eBay, only do so for a fee. These storefronts have a lot of advantages, such as giving you a simple and consolidated way to display all your items at once, custom category names and pages and, in some cases, advanced tools like email marketing and cross-promotional widgets. Even a storefront that isn't free, such as eBay Stores, can be worth it if the discounts and perks of ownership offset the upgrade fee.

There are a lot of reasons why it's a good idea to start selling on your own website instead of on a platform and a myriad of choices of how to do it. It's also the sole topic of one of my other books, *Beyond Amazon, eBay and Etsy: free and low cost alternative marketplaces, shopping cart solutions and e-commerce storefronts*, so I'm not going to repeat myself here. But understand that it's (usually) much more work over selling on a platform, so it's likely better for you to grow into rather than try to use right from the start.

WHAT ABOUT EBAY?

While the SA will get a wide variety of items, a majority will usually be antiques, collectibles and home goods, all of which do particularly well on eBay. While I'm a firm believer in never shackling yourself to a single marketplace, I also don't believe in discounting a platform entirely for any reason, especially if it could be a good fit for your items despite other annoyances. While there's a lot I don't like about the eBay platform, there are several good reasons to consider it for selling your clients' items.

Despite the fact that I'm a multi-channel seller, I list the majority of my Selling Assistant items on eBay. While I take all kinds of items, my specialty is collectibles, especially vintage toys, and I like eBay best for them for several reasons. Firstly, it's still the best place to sell collectibles and vintage items, and it's where you'll get the best prices for what you have to sell as long as you know what you're doing with keywords. Secondly, while I use a mix of Auctions and Fixed Price (I am a great lover of Best Offer), it's hard to beat the auction format for speed.

Items sold via auction are usually gone about a week from when I listed them, so I can pay my client and get on to the next commission. Auctions are also an excellent way to sell a rare or unusual item you aren't sure of the value of since you can just list it and let the market determine its final value through bidding. Of course, on the reverse, auctions can also burn a seller if an item sells for less than expected.

With Fixed Price, be it on eBay or another marketplace, it can take weeks to months for someone to purchase the items, and that's time I can't always afford to waste. As a rule, Fixed Price usually means higher prices but at the expense of speed. It's fine if your client isn't in a rush, and if you've got values already in mind for the items. But clients are rarely patient, and when they've got items where there's no value precedent, auctions are often the best choice.

eBay isn't a perfect selling solution but, to me, the positives outweigh the negatives when it comes to the kind of items I usually sell. That said, I also sell select consignment items via Half.com, Amazon, Craigslist, Etsy and even my own website depending on what they are and what I determine is best for that specific commission. Whether eBay will be a good fit for your service remains to be seen, but I do think it would be a mistake to not give it a try, at least for some items.

SHOULD I SELL FROM MY OWN ACCOUNT OR THE CLIENT'S? WHO WILL BE DOING THE ACTUAL SELLING?

Most Selling Assistant's will want to sell from their own selling accounts whenever possible. This gives you full control over the money, both ingoing and outgoing, and makes it easier for you to manage the post-sale elements like shipping, returns and payment processing. It also means all selling benefits and cross-marketing opportunities go directly back to your accounts.

But while most of this book assumes that you're selling the client's items from your own selling account, there are many reasons why you may opt to sell from the client's account instead. When dealing with a client that's a business or otherwise has a brand of their own to protect, they may prefer you sell their items from a designated storefront themed to their business. Selling from the client's account also lets you avoid some of the annoyances of online selling. Of course, this assumes the client either already has a selling account, that you would create one for them or otherwise require they set one up for this purpose.

How would this even work? Well, first the client would need to give you access to their selling account, and you'd do all the selling for them from there. Or you could just undertake the listing process through their account, then let the client take over and handle all the actual final sale details and shipping themselves. The client would be paying all the selling, payment and shipping costs, as it's their account, but they'd also be getting all the income so you'd need to either bill them for your fee or commission after the fact or just charge a flat fee upfront. While a large corporate client may require this to ensure that that the items are sold under their brand, it can put the SA in a couple of bad situations.

Firstly, because the profits are going directly into the client's account, they'll have to pay you instead of your having all the money and giving them their share after the fact. You'll need to bill your clients for the payment for your service, unless you get that upfront, and, while some small businesses are exemplary, many are slow to pay invoices, often paying late and only after many reminders. While you can probably trust a big company to eventually follow up on an invoice or bill, individuals can be worse. You'll need to make sure you've protected yourself if it goes to small claims court so that you'll get your payment. Chasing up payments isn't just annoying and a time waster, it can really mess up your business when you've got your own bills to pay and can't because your client invoices are still outstanding.

Secondly, it will be the client's account that reaps the benefits of the sales, be that feedback, volume sales discounts, benefits program (such as eBay's Top Rated or PowerSeller) or boosting the sales of your other items. Because the SA isn't getting credit for listing and selling the items, there's less (or no) opportunity to promote your SA service or store while selling. Lastly, if your client isn't selling savvy, it can mean that you'll need to set all or part of their selling account up for them, which can be time-consuming. Just make sure you've set things so that you'll be compensated for any additional work.

There are some advantages to performing your SA service this way if you can put up with the rest. For starters, while their account will get all the benefits, they'll also get any bad feedback, buyer complaints or other negative selling activities that can result, keeping your account untarnished. You also may not want your other items or your business name associated with a particular client or their items, so this extra layer of distance may be more to your preference. If you're just doing the listing and letting the client handle all the details of the final sale, you get yourself out of packing, shipping, returns and dealing with buyers, all of which are some of the most difficult parts of selling.

SHOULD I HAVE A DESIGNATED SELLING ACCOUNT FOR MY SELLING ASSISTANCE SERVICE?

Along the same lines, you may be wondering if you should create a selling account or webstore for your SA items that is separate from your main selling account.

If your designated SA account or store is new and doesn't yet qualify for volume selling benefits like increased search exposure, it can mean lower sale prices for your clients' items than you enjoy on the items listed in the main store. Just as when you sell through the client's account, selling from a separate account means that your other items for sale won't benefit from any cross exposure and your main account won't reap the benefits from the sale of client items. Of course, your account also won't get saddled with any negative selling experiences such as bad feedback or claims that result from client items. It also makes reporting that much easier when all your SA items are segregated into their own account and their fees are not mixed in with your other items. If a client's items are a poor match for the items you usually sell in your main store, you may want to separate them out.

If you predominantly take on SA items that are similar to the items you usually sell for yourself, or if you sell such a wide variety of items that there's nothing that wouldn't really fit in your main store, you probably don't need a new account. But it doesn't need to be an either-or solution. I sell my SA items predominantly in my main storefront, but I do have alternate selling IDs that I use when the occasion arises.

SELLING SUMMARY

Let's take a minute to review your selling situation with a few quick questions.

- Where will you sell?
    - What platforms would be a good fit for the kind of items you sell and also fit your selling needs?
    - Will you be selling across multiple channels?
    - Will you set up a storefront or standalone website or just use a selling account on an existing marketplace?
- How will you sell?
    - Have you practiced selling items as if they were for a client?
    - Will you sell from your own account or the client's?
    - Will you sell from your existing selling account or have a designated one for SA client items?

FEATURES AND UPGRADES

Everything listed in this section is optional. You can run a successful SA business without adding a single feature above a basic selling service, but what will really define your service and set it apart are the features you offer and the ways you upgrade your service above the bare minimum. While you'll likely come up with your own ways to make your service your own, this section will get you started with proven selling points to draw customers to your service.

GOOD CUSTOMER (AND CLIENT) SERVICE

I know, I can't believe I have to list it either, but, believe it or not, customer service is one of the last things many sellers think of as part of their service, and it's one of the biggest things that can hold any business back. Is it really a feature or upgrade? Well, since most of us can probably think of several businesses off the top of our head that continue to thrive despite terrible customer service, treating your customers right isn't technically required to run a business. If you're the only SA in the area, you might be able to get away with being a total jerk and still have a steady stream of customers. But being good to your customers and clients can make a big difference to the success of your business, winning you more loyalty, leading to repeat customers and word-of-mouth marketing.

The best customer service starts as a philosophy you have in mind from the moment you start your business rather than one that you try to shoehorn in after the fact as damage control. It also doesn't need to be as complicated as you might think. After all, most of your customers, especially in the beginning, will be your friends, family and people from your own community, and these are all people you'd want to do right by anyway.

There are also two types of customers you'll be dealing with while running a Selling Assistance service: clients and customers. While both are technically customers, I tend think of "customers" as the buyers who purchase items from your store, whether those items are yours or your clients', while "clients" are the item owners who contract you to do the selling. Is there a different recipe for keeping each group happy?

No matter which kind of customer you're dealing with, you'll want to be sure that you...

- **Have prompt and professional communication.** Always return phone calls and emails promptly. Arrive on time for your client pick-up or call ahead if you're unavoidably running late. Use correct grammar and spelling in all your spoken and writing interactions, and this goes for quick emails and text messages as well as more obvious things like your item description or contracts. Communicate any delays and be upfront about issues. Never resort to personal attacks or other heated dialog.

- **Handle any issues quickly and fairly.** If problems arise, and they will despite your best efforts, deal with them immediately and do your best to resolve them in a way that's fair to your customer. If a buyer's item arrived damaged and they email you about it, every minute that you don't reply they'll get more worried that you're cheating them and more angry. A quick answer, even if it's just to acknowledge that you got the message and are following up, shows the buyer that you care and that you're working on their problem. Using the same example, it wouldn't be fair to tell them that the damaged item is their problem if you're the one who could have packed the item better or insured it. No one ever wants to give a customer their money back, but sometimes it's the right thing to do. In the same way, if your client is angry about how you handled a sale, address it immediately and compensate if needed.

For your store customers, you'll also want to ship your items promptly, package everything well, write clear descriptions, offer a good return policy, and take great item photos. For clients, you'll need to fulfill your contracted promises, sell their items to the best of your abilities, honor their requests and address their fears and concerns with confidence. In a way, it involves wearing two different hats because what's good for your business isn't necessarily good for your customers, and you'll need to decide when to prioritize the needs of one over the other.

That said, never underestimate the power of an apology and, failing that, a partial refund. Sometimes just a genuine "I'm sorry," even if you're certain that you weren't the one in the wrong, can smooth over a situation to where there's no need for any additional compensation. And while you'll often need to issue full refunds or give extras as the only way to fix a bad situation, you'll be amazed at how often people are satisfied with just a partial refund, even if it's only a few dollars. With many angry customers, it's the principle of the thing more than the money itself, and a little humility and a few dollars on your part can make it all go away with surprising ease.

Good customer service doesn't need to be complicated. Just use the good old Golden Rule: *Do unto others as you would have them do unto you.* In any dealing with a customer or client, just put yourself in their position and treat them as you would want to be treated in that situation. In some cases, you may need to tweak this since something that wouldn't bother you may bother your customers, and you'll need to adjust accordingly, but it'll still give you a great foundation to work from. And while it may drive you crazy to have to give a refund or go the extra mile for that pain-in-the-butt customer that's being a thorn in your side, remember, an unhappy customer can do serious damage to your business through bad word of mouth. An unhappy customer that you win back around, however, can turn into not only one of your best customers but also give back a hundred fold through good word of mouth.

PO BOX OR OTHER LOCKED MAILBOXES

Now that sites like eBay limit buyers from paying via checks and money orders, it's tempting to forget snail mail, but regular postal mail still plays a part in any business. Not only will your business need to establish an official address for correspondence, forms and other paperwork, you'll also still be accepting returns and exchanges through the physical mail.

While the rest of the world increasingly goes digital, the government on both the national and state level is still maddeningly attached to paper and has been slow to adapt.

You may be fine with giving out your address, especially if you have a retail location with drop-off hours, but many sellers are uncomfortable letting their customers know their personal address when running a home-based business. Think about it: posting a message on your storefront that your store is on vacation right next to your home address is like asking for people to come and rob you!

Another concern is privacy. Your business will be getting a variety of very important documents, especially at tax time. Is your home address secure enough to ensure that none of these items are misplaced or stolen?

When you register your business, you'll also be giving out your address on a variety of forms. Many of these forms will be public record. Wouldn't you rather have a more private mail option with features for added convenience and professionalism rather than splash your home address everywhere?

The simplest solution is to get a locked mailbox. A Post Office Box, commonly abbreviated as PO Box, is a locked mailbox available at your local post office in a variety of sizes for a yearly fee. Your rental will include a key that ensures that you are the only person who can access your box. You can also opt to get an email or text message whenever you get new mail so you don't need to waste a trip to an empty box.

But before you run down to the post office, also consider retail options such as Pakmail, Mail Boxes etc. and PostNet. These are just three of the many storefronts that rent mailboxes. They often offer additional features that the USPS does not and are sometimes cheaper. Most are also drop-off locations for not only USPS but also FedEx and UPS. If you frequently ship using these methods, a mailbox in a retail location such as these could save you a trip.

An added feature of nearly all locked mailboxes is that they offer street address shipping. In other words, they allow you to use the physical mailing address of the location where your box is housed instead of the PO Box 123 format. Not only is this handy when you want to look more professional and give a physical mailing address instead of a box number, it allows you to have items delivered by UPS, FedEx and others that otherwise cannot ship to a locked mailbox. Many will even let you keep a signature on file so they can sign for packages on your behalf.

That said, for all the advantages, locked mailboxes can be expensive. While there are advantages to going with a retail location over the USPS, will that retail location still be there in a year, after you've gone to the trouble of putting your new box address on all your business cards? For that matter, with the way the Postal Service is doing, is your post office any more or less likely to stay open?

You can run a SA business quite successfully without getting a private mailbox, but it's a small expense I would recommend investing in. It's certainly not a perfect option, but as it's only one of the ways to protect your mail and home address, it's worth looking into. I've had a PO Box through my local post office for years, and I've found be well worth the cost.

DESIGNATE A BUSINESS PHONE LINE

Does your SA business need a phone number? You aren't required to have one. You can also just use your existing home or cell phone number. That said, there are a lot of advantages to getting a designated phone line for your SA business.

Many of the details of your business and domain registration will be public record, and nearly all require a phone number. Wouldn't you prefer to have the designated business line be the one that's public and not your personal cell or home phone?

Professionalism is another thing to consider. Your voicemail can often be the very first contact a customer has with your company, and that alone can win or lose their business in a minute. An informal voicemail message may be fine for your home phone, but it will turn off a client who wants to believe they're dealing with a business, not just some random guy (or gal). A designated phone line gives you the opportunity to record a business specific voicemail message with details like your hours, website, email address and anything else you want to include to give a professional first impression. A business line also allows you to know when you pick it up that a client is on the other end, avoiding awkward informal greetings or the dreaded less than ideal receptionist such as a child.

A phone number for your business can also be a selling point for anyone uncomfortable with email or technology, as many SA clients are. Many Selling Assistants do not offer phone support, as they deal primarily online. Your phone line could be the extra that attracts a less tech-savvy customer to you over your competitors.

The ability to talk to a human, even over the phone, can inspire more trust. Sometimes just having a voice to connect with your name is enough to secure you their business. People simply feel more comfortable trusting their items and future dollars to someone they've spoken to and feel like they know. Many of my initial SA client contacts happen over the phone and then, after that first conversation, they opt to switch to email communication or text.

While email or texting may seem like the more logical and convenient method of contact to you, consider having a phone line for those clients who'd prefer more old-fashioned communication.

BEYOND THE LANDLINE

A designated cell or landline can be pricey. I'll let you into a little secret that has served me very well over the years. VOIP and internet-based phone numbers aren't just cheaper, they often give you more features and flexibility than a landline ever could.

My business number is actually a telephone number I

have through Skype. It only costs me a single yearly fee that is less than a single month of a normal phone line. When a client calls that number, they are actually calling the Skype software on my computer. If I'm working, I answer the call through my computer headset as if it were a normal phone call. If I'm not at my computer, it goes to the voicemail that comes with the number.

Skype is only one of many similar options out there. Google Voice is another and, at present, they offer both incoming and outgoing calls for free. AOL will also give you a phone number for free, though you can lose it if you forget to log in on a certain timetable, which can be a real pain if you've already started using it on official forms. If you decide to go this route, look for a service that's reliable and lets you pick your own phone number. Some even let you choose individual digit combinations if you want to create a memorable number. When you're running a local business like a SA service, having a phone number with a local area code is very important even if that number is a virtual one and not really in the area. Clients will never know they're not calling a local number and still pay local rates as if they were. It also makes your business seem closer to them, and that gives them a better perception of you right from the start.

Clients often call at all hours of the day or night because they think you're working out of an office and don't realize it's actually your home. Some clients can also be annoying, calling all the time. Because my phone is through software on my PC, the phone doesn't ring and disturb anyone in my house if I'm not available to answer. This allows me to run an international business and never worry about getting woken or disturbed by unwanted calls. Your number will also work on most smartphones and every computer or tablet, meaning I always have my business phone with me, so it's as good as a designated business cell phone but uses whatever you're already carrying. It can also do text messaging, video chat, instant messaging and caller ID if you need those features. Most also have the option to forward calls to the normal phone of my choice whenever needed. All this for much, much less than a cell or landline.

From the perspective of your customers, an internet-based phone number works exactly the same as a normal phone line, but from your end, it gives you more flexibility and substantial savings over a designated land or cell line. That said, none of the services listed above are a perfect option. You'll want to do your own research to find what best fits your needs and look into phone line options both traditional and non.

PICK-UP TERMS

The most common way to secure items from clients is to go and pick them up. This can happen at the client's home or at a previously arranged public meeting point. This is only practical if the person is within a reasonable driving distance, but most of your clients will be local anyway.

Offering pick-up with your service is a major selling point, as it involves the least amount of work on the client's part. All they need to do is get the box of stuff ready and hand it to you. The less work something is to do, the more likely people will actually do it, so for many potential clients, offering pick-up can be the main feature that makes the deal for you.

A few things to consider when going to pick up items from a client:

- You want to look neat and professional, but traditional business attire such as a suit or skirt is a little over the top for most pick-ups. Though it is your first client contact, you'll also likely be doing some heavy lifting. Most of what you will be handling will be dirty, dusty and otherwise messy, so a neat shirt (no inappropriate sayings) and pants, possibly even nice jeans, are likely fine.

- Make sure whatever vehicle you bring will have room enough to carry all the items you are picking up. You'll want to clean out your trunk ahead of time as well. It is very unprofessional to force your client to wait as you tidy up. You should have a sense of the volume of items you'll be picking up before you go, so you'll know ahead of time if you need to secure another, larger, vehicle.

- Make it clear to the client that they will need to have the items ready for you to take. In other words, you should not have to climb into their attic and fetch the boxes yourself, nor should you have to sort through a box of books for that one rare edition they want you to sell. They should have them either waiting for you outside or in another reasonably accessible location, already sorted.

- At the risk of sounding like your mother, please take caution when entering the house of a complete stranger. Make sure your loved ones know where you are and try to bring someone else along with you if possible. If you are uncomfortable with the situation, arrange to meet the client in a public place to collect the items.

DROP-OFF HOURS

If you're not willing to go to the client to get their items, then they'll need to be able to get them to you. Drop-off hours are another great feature to add to your service. These can be a regular block of hours that you're always available for clients to drop by or just appointments that you schedule as needed client by client. Offering drop-offs can be easier for you because you don't need to drive anywhere to pick up or transport the items. It can also make your business seem more professional and give potential clients more confidence in your service because they'll get to see your physical location instead of just your car.

Anywhere you offer drop-offs, make sure to provide the client with some kind of receipt that you did receive their item so they have a written record of the transaction. Also, when setting up drop-off hours, don't just offer the standard 9 to 5. Most potential clients will want to drop off items either before or after work, so extend your hours beyond the normal work week.

Maintaining regularly scheduled drop-off hours can also

encourage walk-up business. Allowing walk-ups is the easiest way to ensnare the spontaneous client that operates on the spur of the moment. Imagine the weekend warrior who, full of the zeal of having just cleaned out the garage or attic, wants to come and hand off her items at that very moment to be rid of them. That kind of person doesn't necessarily have the patience or forethought to arrange time with an SA ahead of time and may love the instant nature of just showing up, signing away their items to you right then, and moving on with their lives.

If you've got a public-ready space in your home, such as an office or locked lobby, that's the ideal solution. Another option is to have a physical retail storefront. If you're working out of your home, drop-offs can be tricky.

Do you want strangers stopping off at your personal residence? For that matter, do you want potential clients seeing your home? Are you comfortable advertising the address of your home in your SA marketing materials, letting the general public know that you store other people's valuables at your house? Can you handle SA drop-offs to your home in a way that still makes your company come off professionally? It can absolutely be done, it just involves a little planning. If you do decide to offer drop-off hours at your home, please make sure to take additional security precautions, as it can present a danger to both your privacy and personal safety if you're not careful.

You'll also need to consider security on the client's end. How can you ensure the safety of their items in the event of loss or damage once in your possession? If your drop-off station is unmanned, how will you handle items you aren't willing to sell or items that were misrepresented? Can people just drop things off without singing a contract first?

Any drop-off location, whether in your home or not, should be staffed during drop-off hours. You'll likely need to hire someone to run the drop-off location when you aren't available. This may also involve training that person on what kind of items to accept because otherwise you'll be stuck selling whatever they commit to on your behalf.

If you can't find a way to offer drop-offs with your current situation, consider starting a partnership with a local business that will accept drop-offs on your behalf. This partnership could even be done in exchange for your selling their items for them or some other barter. Even if you have to pay some kind of monthly fee or strike some other financial deal in order to mooch some of their counter space from time to time, it'll be far less than you'd pay to have your own storefront. Just keep in mind that the location you partner with will reflect on your business. If the person manning their counter is rude to your customer, or if the storefront is in an unsavory location, that will taint how your business is perceived. That said, if there's a local business that is similar in nature to what you sell, it could be a big boost in business for both of you.

LET CLIENTS SHIP THEIR ITEMS TO YOU

Even if you already offer pick-ups and/or drop-off hours, you may want to expand the reach of your service even farther. Allowing clients to ship their items to you opens your business up in a big way. Now anyone with access to postal mail can be your client, meaning you could offer your SA services on the national or even global level. Of course, local clients may also take advantage of your shipping service, as it may be easier for them to pop their items in the mail instead of having you come out for a pick-up or them go out for a drop-off.

There are a few things to consider, however. Firstly, who will pay the shipping costs? Your services would be that much more attractive if you let clients bill the shipping costs to your shipper's account, but do you really want to take on those extra costs? If the items are worth enough and covering shipping seals the deal, it may be well worth it to secure the contract.

Can people just send you items without first contacting you or signing a contract? If no, what if they do anyway? Letting people just send you stuff without first requiring contact or contract can mean more business, but it can also mean just getting a bunch of stuff you can't sell that now you're stuck with.

But even if you specify not to send anything until they've been approved, clients may anyway. Us humans are not always known for paying a ton of attention to directions, and the lure of just putting your stuff in a box and getting money back magically is pretty strong.

And what if things go wrong? What happens if the client's items arrive broken or get lost in the mail? What if the client sends you items that they misrepresented? Not getting to physically see the items before committing to them can be dangerous, and you'll want to make sure you're protected.

That big list of questions isn't meant to scare you off but rather to get you thinking of how you want to handle this feature if you decide to offer it. I accept clients from around the world, and many ship their items to me, though I do require that we have a contract first so that my business is protected. If you've got a specialty that's a certain niche, you may want to open yourself up to a wider client base who would gladly go through the hassle of packing and shipping if it meant that their items could benefit from your specific expertise. For example, My Little Pony toys are one of our biggest focuses, and it's not uncommon for us to take clients from far away who ship their My Little Pony items to us because they know we can get a better price for them than a local seller without our product knowledge.

MULTI-LANGUAGE SUPPORT

If you are already bi or multi-lingual, then this is a simple upgrade for your business. If you only speak one language, however, you may wish to hire a translator when needed for clients that speak something other than you. What languages should you support? This depends on your area.

If you work out of an area with a large minority population, it's foolish not to court them for your services, especially since they're a segment that small businesses often overlook. Beyond having a translator on hand to give them a way to communicate with you in their preferred tongue, you may also want to offer alternate language versions of your website, contract, and marketing materials. Hiring a freelancer to translate these for you isn't difficult or expensive if you use services like Fiverr, oDesk or Elance, and it could double your customer base if done correctly. Actively targeting a language that others ignore can give you an advantage over the competition, particularly in cities were ethnicities are clustered together.

SPECIALIZATION

Many Selling Assistants will sell almost anything. Over time, you'll become adept at a wide variety of items and know at a glance how best to sell them. But as you become more experienced as a SA, or if you just want to provide a different service from your competition, you may want to consider offering a specialization. Keep in mind, however, that if you indicate that you specialize in something, you may be accidentally sending clients without that type of item away because they'll assume that's all you sell. Consider creating two separate SA profiles if you wish to indicate that, while you will sell anything, you're a specialist for this one particular type of item.

There are three main reasons for offering a specialization.

- **Distinguish yourself from other Selling Assistants.** If there are other Selling Assistants in the area that will sell anything and everything, you might want to offer a more specialized service in a specific area such as antiques, toys or new-with-tag items. Similarly, if the only other SA in town specializes in one area, you may want to focus on a different type of item.

- **Take advantage of your expertise.** If you are particularly skilled at, knowledgeable about, or have strong marketing connections in a particular field, then you can offer a superior service to clients with items of that type. For example, if you run a popular website or blog on stamp collecting, your specialization is a big selling point to the client with stamps because you not only know your stuff but can also promote their listings to your established audience. If your existing webstore already has a strong focus, that's another reason to seek out items that fit with what you're already selling.

- **Follow your passions.** Work is more like play when you're doing something you love, isn't it? If there's something you're particularly passionate about and prefer to work on because it's in line with your interests, you may want to consider listing it as a specialization. This ensures that you'll get more clients with the type of items you enjoy selling, making working with them that much more of a joy.

If your specialization turns out to be lucrative enough, you may have the luxury of focusing only on those items. Then you can work on expanding your reach, offering your SA services to your specific niche on a national or even global level. While narrowing your service down to a single category of item does limit your potential client pool, it may result in more loyalty from the buyers and clients you do have because they value your focus.

CHARITY AND NON-PROFIT LISTINGS

Advertising that you specialize in charity or non-profit listings is a simple way to attract more business, particularly from non-profits and charities themselves. Fundraisers for local events or just individuals looking for a way to give back without having to open their pocketbooks will both be drawn to this. The best part, for you, is that this feature doesn't involve a lot of work to add to your service.

Specializing in charity or non-profit listings can mean any or all of the following:

- **You'll sell a client's items through a service such as eBay's Giving Works, which allows you to**

automatically funnel a percentage of the final sale price of any item directly to the non-profit of their choice. If you've never done this before, it's actually just a single option on the listing form, so it only takes a moment more than a normal listing. Once the items sells, you'll get your payment from the buyer as usual, but Giving Works will automatically bill you for their percentage. (Note that since a service like Giving Works takes the donation upfront, you'll need to bill your client for things like selling and payment fees separately, as you won't have the money from the item sale to subtract them from.)

- **You'll help a non-profit to get set up on services like Giving Works, if they aren't already, so others can sell items and give a percentage back to them.** This process sounds more complicated than it is and is actually just a bit of paperwork. But you may also want to create some verbiage for the non-profit for their handouts and website explaining the process to their donors as part of your service since many people aren't even aware of this way to give, let alone familiar with how to use it.

- **You'll sell items for a non-profit or individual and then donate the profits after the fact on their behalf.** Instead of issuing a check to the client at the end of the contract, you'll send it directly to the non-profit of their choice in their name.

- **You'll act as a Selling Assistant for a fundraiser.** The party looking to raise funds would have their members donate items, services, or experiences. They would then give you everything that was donated and you would list it all like you would a normal client's items. The difference is that you'll likely list them all at the same time, and the organization will probably want you to list them via Auction format instead of Fixed Price to allow for bidding. That would allow the non-profit to promote all the listings at once to their membership and also be able to accept bids both from local patrons, as they would in a silent auction or other local event, and the entire rest of the world at the same time, greatly increasing their potential profits. All proceeds, after fees and your cut, will go back to the original organization.

These are just some ideas to get you started. Marketing yourself as non-profit or fundraiser-friendly is really not much more work than what you're already doing with a normal SA contract, but it opens up your business a host of new customers such as schools, social clubs, church groups, and more. Just make sure you still make a profit when you want to. While donating your time to a cause you feel passionate about is great, make sure the non-profit knows when you *do* expect to be compensated for your work.

SELLER TRAINING AND TUTORING

What if we took the term "Selling Assistance" a little more literally? For some clients, instead of taking their items and selling for them, what if you actually sat down and helped them list the items themselves? You'd charge for this training, of course, either a flat fee or hourly rate.

If a customer contacts you with items you aren't willing to sell, wouldn't it be nice to still have a way to earn some money from them? Steering a customer into hiring you to help them do the listings themselves instead of you doing the selling is a great way to turn a potentially negative relationship into a positive one. Instead of parting ways after a contract, even former clients could transition into your tutoring and still be a source of income. Offering seller training opens up your business to a whole new population as many more people want to learn about selling online than already have a specific item ready to sell.

As they've already got the selling expertise, many SAs also opt to offer tutoring for would-be sellers as a supplemental income. This could be as large as a whole class full of people or one-on-one lessons with individuals. Workshops can be in person or over the web from the comfort of everyone's own home. Keep in mind that you can usually charge more for private lessons, though you may be earning multiple fees from each student in a class.

eBay offers an authorized program, eBay Education Specialists, for those that want to offer eBay-certified seller training with more official-looking credentials. I know several SAs that are registered eBay Education Specialists, even though they never actually teach or offer tutoring, simply because they think it looks better to have eBay's seal of approval on their marketing materials. While the eBay program gives your selling expertise a little more weight and provides you with some useful tools, it can be costly, and then you're limited to eBay's agreement. Really, anyone can offer seller training without joining any program, and then you can teach on your own terms.

Even if you have no interest in doing paid lessons, teaching the occasional free class at a local space such as a library is a great way to attract customers to your service. There's nothing like realizing how much work selling online really is to inspire you to hire someone else to do it! Which is why you shouldn't ever worry about seller training putting you out of a job. Many of the people you train will, upon trying it themselves, decide it's well worth your fee or commission to let you sell their items after all.

OFFER CLIENTS THEIR OWN STOREFRONT OR SELLING ACCOUNT

While the majority of your clients will only have a single batch of items that they want you to sell and then they're done, some, particularly corporate clients, crafters and other local businesses, may have a continuous stream of items for you to sell. In that case, it may make sense to offer them their own personalized storefront or selling account. For a predetermined fee, you'd get them set up for selling and then either sell their items for them from this new account or hand the account over to them and let them take over the sales.

Alternately, you could have a designated storefront that

you customize to each client for just the term of their contract, and once their items are sold, you recycle it for the next one.

EMPLOYEES AND OTHER HELP

As your business grows, there's going to be a point when you can't handle the volume of work on your own. In the beginning, you may just enlist a friend or family member to assist you in exchange for a favor or two, but at some point, you'll want to check with your local government about how adding paid help would affect your business. You can add employees whether you're a home-based business or a retail store, and these could be locals who come to work in person or telecommuters who do their work for you over the internet. The actual process of adding employees to your business can vary widely depending on where you are, so you should consult with local government on how to get started.

It can be a complicated process. It's more than just additional responsibilities and paperwork. There are things like health insurance, worker's comp, required posted notices, and more you'll need to familiarize yourself with. Many SAs also have a confidentiality or non-disclosure agreement or even competition clauses drawn up that they require employees to sign as a guarantee that someone they train won't turn around and steal their customers to start their own, rival business.

Another option, instead of hiring a full or part-time employee, is to hire a contractor. While this is simpler from a paperwork standpoint, as a contractor can usually be paid out of your billing system and does not require a payroll, there are limitations and specifications on what a contractor can and cannot do before they become an employee. Failure to adhere to these guidelines can result in fees and other penalties.

While you'll want to do your own research, if you're looking to hire someone for continuing work, such as a regular hourly shift listing items for you that you'll directly oversee, you'll usually want an employee. If you need someone for a specific project and care only about the result, i.e. that the work is done as directed, not how it is done, then a contractor may be the better option. Keep in mind that a contractor doesn't have to be a one and done situation. If you find a contractor you like, you can always open a new contract whenever you have new work for them.

But, intimidating as bringing on more help may be, it'll usually be worth it. The one thing you'll hear all the most successful sellers echo is that their business increased exponentially once they hired some help. Not only will more hands give you the chance to get more work done, it will also free you up personally to do more than just the grunt work of photographing and listing. How could your business grow if you had more time to work on the big stuff?

Vet potential employees carefully and go for the best offer, not the cheapest one. Another thing I would caution you against is going lightly into business with friends or family. It's tempting when you need help and someone you know needs a job to just jump in, but it takes a special type of finesse from both parties to make this scenario work. While it may end up being great, chances are either your relationship or business will suffer, so be cautious with your hiring, interviewing every candidate thoroughly even if you think you already know them. And should your first hiring experience be a poor one, don't let that sour you on the whole idea. Learn from your mistakes and choose more wisely the next time around.

The one thing I do have to stress, however, is don't try to pay your workers "under the table." "Under the table" is an expression that refers to employment that isn't reported to the government. I can't think of anywhere this isn't illegal, as it's tax evasion, but many SAs engage in this practice anyway for a variety of reasons. When you pay under the table, your workers aren't employees in any legal sense, and you'd likely be paying them in an untraceable method like cash.

Even if it wasn't illegal and not worth the hundreds of risks to you and your business, I wouldn't recommend this practice anyway because by paying off the record, you're only cheating yourself in the long run by hiding an expense and making yourself look like you're making more than you actually are.

BRICK AND MORTAR: BEYOND THE HOME-BASED BUSINESS

While you'll likely want to start your business out of your home, one of the biggest upgrades you can add to your service is a physical storefront. Whether this means you renovate part of your home to be a professional public space for meeting clients or you rent a retail location at a local strip mall, it involves a host of additional challenges beyond what we've already discussed.

The advantages of having a physical storefront are many. It gives your business greater visibility, which can be a big help with marketing, and makes it more attractive to customers, as most view a storefront as having more permanence and professionalism. You'll get more walk-up clients, and it allows you the freedom to offer a host of other upgrades such as selling items in your physical store, hosting classes or workshops, and having regular drop-off hours, etc. Having your own space can give you freedom over running the business out of your home.

However, with this freedom comes a bunch of new complications. If you're renting a space, you'll need to factor those additional costs into your bottom line, and that's not simply rent but also things like utilities and insurance. There's maintenance to consider as well. While no one's the wiser if you work out of a messy home office, appearances matter to customers, and you'll need to keep your store clean and in good repair. You'll also need help to cover the storefront when you're not available or to staff the counter while you're doing other work.

Only you know how much profit your business makes and whether your income is enough to sustain a brick and mortar location. But it's a huge leap from running a home-based business to a retail storefront, and I would suggest that you wait until you've been working as a SA full time for a while before even considering getting a physical location. This way you'll know that you're making an educated decision and have enough experience with the process to know if it's worth the gamble. Your business income can vary wildly from year to year, and you want to make sure you're not basing your entire decision on a year that was a onetime fluke.

Many SAs with physical storefronts also add additional services such as print and copy services, serving as UPS and FedEx drop-off centers, locked mailbox rentals, distribution, notary public, etc. All of these can be additional moneymakers and another draw to get clients in the door, but they also come with their own expenses and complications. Are you ready to go into a totally different sort of business on the side?

I can tell you that I have been making the majority of my income on eBay for just over a decade and a half, and I still work predominantly out of my home. Because of the flexibility of the SA program, I can adjust my workload to ensure that it's never more than my staff and I can handle, and I have never seen the need to move into a retail storefront, particularly when I can make the money without the extra hassles and expense. A variety of physical Selling Assistance locations in my immediate area have come and gone, but that has never stopped my flow of business.

But if making that leap could increase your business, you shouldn't fear it just because it's a big change.

FRANCHISES

If you do decide to get a physical storefront, you may not have to start from zero. When the eBay Trading Assistant program was active, there were dozens of Selling Assistance companies that offered franchise opportunities, and many still thrive today, though the eBay Drop-Off Location program itself is long gone. A franchise offers you the opportunity to join an established brand that might help you not only to clear the hurdle of buyer trust, but also to join a proven system rather than starting from nothing. Some of these franchises have become well known, so the strength of their name gives you another advantage. They can also help you with some of the hardest parts of running a brick and mortar SA business such as securing financing and navigating auctioneering laws. The most popular eBay Selling Assistance franchise opportunity in the USA is iSoldit (http://www.i-soldit.com/), but there are others with a strong regional presence, so you'll want to do some research to find the best option in your area.

The advantage of becoming part of a franchise is that they'll get you started with a method, software and policies to help your service run smoothly right at the start instead of your having to discover what works over time. The downsides are that there are often franchise fees, and you may find yourself trapped by corporate policies you don't agree with. If you enjoy the freedom of designing your own service, a franchise probably isn't for you. If you're keen on opening a brick and mortar location, however, it'd be foolish not to at least investigate your franchise options because it could mean the difference between success and failure.

COMPETITION, COLLABORATION AND THE TRUST FACTOR

One thing that we haven't discussed in great detail is competition, and that's because it can vary drastically from area to area. You may find that you're the only practicing SA within a 50-mile radius, that you are the only individual Selling Assistant but that there is a brick and mortar consignment shop in town, or that there are 3 SAs on your street alone. There are actually thousands of sellers offering SA services just like yours all over the world right now, but that shouldn't deter you. There's plenty of business to go around and distinguishing yourself from the others is not as difficult as you might think.

The two biggest things that potential clients are looking for in a SA are trust and price, and often in that order. Price is self-explanatory: how much of their profit will they have to surrender to you. Everything else equal, of course they'll go with the person charging a 20% commission over the one charging a 50% one.

Trust is less obvious. From the perspective of a client, having a random stranger they met on the internet come to their house and drive off with all of their stuff is shady. The more you can do to give them a feeling of security and confidence in you and your service, the more likely they are to hire you. It may come down to a single gut feeling they had about how you speak over the phone, dress to meet with them, the number of typos on your website or other seemingly irrelevant details, which is why you always want to present yourself professionally and in the best possible light. But that need for trust is so great that clients are often willing to agree to a higher fee or commission with someone they trust more than to go for the bargain with someone they don't feel comfortable giving their items to.

Any brick and mortar location usually has the advantage in buyer trust because of their physical location, but an SA working from home can usually best them by a good deal on price. A retail location will have more overhead and will therefore need to charge more to break even, and that really evens the playing field. In a similar way, a Selling Assistant that's been in business for decades may have built up a lot of local loyalty but may only specialize in a few types of items, leaving you to sell everything else. Even another SA on your block will not affect you that much if you both have different specialties.

You are in complete control of the terms of your service and have the opportunity to customize what you offer to directly compete with the others in your area. It is entirely possible for several SAs to thrive in an immediate area, and in the end, it will be the quality and focus of your service that sets you apart from the others. Every Selling Assistant not only has their own policies and fees, but they also have their own niche, restrictions and time constraints, the gaps in which leave room for you to find your place even in an already crowded area. If you're the only SA in town who offers that feature I need, be it speaking another language, offering pick-up, or something else, you'll win my business.

That said, instead of being at war with each other, you may have better success building up a partnership or at least a friendship with any other local SAs. This could be as simple as offering to refer any clients that you can't take on either because you're already overwhelmed with work or because they have items you're not interested in selling. Might you eventually join forces and split the workload? Could you subcontract each other for some extra help in times of need? Better yet, could you combine your marketing efforts, splitting the cost of ads and press?

Even if you never end up interacting with another SA in your area, the important thing is not to view them as enemies. As long as you're welcoming, friendly and professional in all your dealings with them, you'll likely find them to be the same. If not, it's no trouble to ignore them, and your business will still thrive.

EXTERNAL WEBSITE, PROFESSIONALLY-DESIGNED LOGO OR COMPANY BLOG

If you have graphic or web design skills, some quick and easy upgrades to make your service more professional is to design yourself a professional-looking website with an official logo for your company. In this digital age, your website is the first impression potential clients will get of your business and can serve as a brochure for what you offer. A good logo isn't just memorable, it shapes how your clients view your business before you exchange a single word. And the benefits of having a blog both to market your services and attract customers as well as to help potential clients find your website with better search placement are well known.

But having something that's badly designed can sometimes do more damage than having nothing at all. If you don't have the skills to create something yourself, you may need to hire someone to make sure it's done right, which will be an extra expense. How much of an expense can vary to anywhere from $5 from a site like Fiverr to hundreds depending on what you have in mind.

That said, before you look into hiring a designer, take a look at some of the free website templates and themes out there. Something like the free blogging software from Wordpress.org or even a Blogger or Tumblr site comes with a variety of slick-looking free templates that can make your site look great at no extra cost. Sure, you won't be the only person using that particular look, so it's not as good as a customized design just for you, but it's better to be plain than have a site so ugly it's a customer turn-off.

You can get free hosting and blogging software through a variety of platforms, the aforementioned Blogger, Tumblr or even Wordpress.com (which is different than .org) are just three of many, but that hosting will have limitations and restrictions on how you use it. Paying for hosting will give you more freedom but may be an extra expense you don't really need if your site is small. No matter which way you decide to go, registering your domain name is inexpensive and a good thing to do.

I ran my SA business for many years before I found the need for a logo, external website or blog, but as soon as I had them, they increased business dramatically. These are all things that you may decide to add later on as your business grows and changes. That said, you may discover that there's a discount if you purchase website hosting at the same time as your domain name or that designing marketing materials is easier if you already have a logo to use, so it's worth considering.

FEATURES AND UPGRADES REVIEW

Let's take a quick second look at all the add-ons we considered to enhance your business in this section.

- Good customer service to ensure good reviews and positive word of mouth.

- A locked mailbox to keep your mail private and your correspondence professional.

- Designated phone line, even if it's only an internet-based phone number, to entice less tech-savvy clients.

- Offering a pick-up service for your clients' items.

- Providing regular or scheduled drop-off hours at staffed counter.

- Accepting client items via postal mail to entice out-of-area clients drawn to your expertise.

- Support and marketing materials in additional languages to court local minority populations.

- Designating a specialization in a type of item you're particularly knowledgeable about.

- Providing special selling and listing services for non-profits, fundraisers and other charities.

- Offering tutoring or training services to court customers with nothing to sell but who would still like to learn about the process.

- Provide clients with their own customized selling account or storefront.

- Hire employees or contract workers to share the workload, freeing you to work on other aspects of the business.

- Opening a brick and mortar location, either independently or affiliated with an existing franchise.

- Cultivate a good relationship with other local Selling Assistants and keep competition friendly, or even partner with them for profitable collaborations.

- Create an external website, company blog or have a professionally designed logo to give your brand a memorable look.

WHAT WILL YOUR SERVICE LOOK LIKE?

This section gave you a lot to think about, but hopefully you've been taking notes about your decisions and starting to get a sense of what your service will be like. Once you've decided how you'll profit and handle other financial matters, where and how you'll do the actual selling and what features you'll add to set your service apart, read over what you've chosen and try to see how everything will fit together. You may discover problems or opportunities when looking at the elements side by side that you didn't notice when considering them individually.

Of course, nothing you decided here is final. As you begin to offer your service, your business will grow, adapt and change as needed. You'll always add and remove elements of your business as you go, but at least now you've got something to start with.

With this first picture in our heads of what our business could be like, now it's time to get started...

STARTING YOUR SELLING ASSISTANCE BUSINESS

Sounds simple enough, right? Selling items for other people and maybe customizing with a few extras. You're on it. But prior to diving into the actual selling, we have to do some planning.

Before you start any business, you want to make sure that you're two things: organized and protected. Organized because otherwise you'll waste a lot of time and money spinning your wheels because you didn't have a plan. Protected to make sure you don't find yourself in legal trouble either with clients or the government come tax time.

GOING LEGIT: BUSINESS NAMES & REGISTRATION

Many people start an online business with some confused idea that they'll be able to keep the income under the table by not reporting it and not pay taxes on it. This is never the case. According to the IRS, you must report any income made, and that includes income from internet marketplaces like eBay, Etsy or even Craigslist. Both the sites themselves and payment processors such as PayPal do their own reporting to the IRS, and the debate rages daily on how that will increase in the future. Even as the system operates now, most Selling Assistants find themselves in a volume program such as Top Rated or PowerSellers based on the volume of items that they sell for other people, which tells anyone who looks at your account that you are making at least $12,000 a year.

The income you make from online sales is too public to hide. You're just asking for tax penalties and audits. But that's actually fine.

That instinct to hide your income from the government is misplaced. You're only thinking about dodging income tax while missing the bigger picture. Registering as a business will actually save you money on taxes in the long run and help you keep more of your profits. Regardless of the size of your business, be it part time or full time, there are several big advantages to registering your SA services as a business.

- **Businesses are allowed to claim more expenses then private citizens on their personal taxes.** All the packing supplies (boxes, bubble wrap, tape, etc.), marketing materials (flyers, postcards, PPC ads, etc.), fees (selling fees, eBay Store subscription, PayPal fees, website or domain name hosting, etc.) and other purchases you make for the business are taken into account before you report your income. In addition to the obvious purchases, a business can also claim less obvious expenses such as the cost of your digital camera, desk chair, dedicated phone line, computer, clothing you wear for client meetings, mileage for your car when driving to client meet-ups and even a percentage of your household bills and mortgage, provided these expenses occurred within the year that you are reporting.

- **The income you report to the government takes your expenses into account.** When reporting your income as a private citizen, if you took $5,000 of income in from eBay, that is what you'd have to report even though

$2,000 of it may be the cost of start-up and supplies. When reporting as a business, you would only be taxed on the $3,000 of actual income and not the expenses. In turn, as an SA, if you sell a vintage clock for $1,000 on Etsy, based on your sales record, it looks like you just made $1,000. If you were selling that item for a client at a 20% commission, you really only made $200 with the other $800 going to the client, PayPal and Etsy for fees. With a registered business, it's easier to keep a paper trail of that transaction to prove you should only be taxed on the $200, not the full $1,000. And if your expenses are greater than your income and you lose money, you not only won't pay taxes... you'll usually get a break.

- **Extra tax incentives exist for businesses.** There's no tax break just for being a woman, but there are tax breaks and other incentives for female-owned companies. The same applies for businesses run by minority groups and for those that operate out of areas that are trying to court small business. Research the programs in your state, and you may be surprised at the ways businesses get extra help where individuals don't.

There are some other challenges to tax reporting if you report as a private citizen. As soon as you make greater than $1,000 for the year, you should talk to your tax professional and start making quarterly estimated tax payments. As most online income has nothing withheld, in many states, you will face a penalty on your year-end income taxes if your profit exceeds $1,000. For more information on when you may need to consider filing your taxes quarterly to avoid paying a penalty, consult with your accountant and visit the official IRS website at http://www.irs.gov.

If you don't currently have an accountant, now is an excellent time to find one. Many will give you a free consultation in exchange for your business come tax time. While you can certainly do your own business taxes, having a professional do it, at least for the first year, is a very good idea.

REGISTERING YOUR BUSINESS AND BUSINESS NAME

HOW DO YOU ACTUALLY REGISTER A BUSINESS?

The process of registering a business varies depending on your country and even from state to state within the US. Consult your local state government for the specifics in your area. While there are many different kinds of businesses, and the registration process will vary based on your state, registering is a relatively simple process and usually costs under $100, so it's in an inexpensive investment in the future of your company.

Your local government's website should walk you through the process and even let you submit online, so it's fairly painless to do yourself. If the process is overwhelming or if your local administration is less than helpful, there is also a variety of companies that will file the paperwork for you for a fee.

While you will want to make sure you do your own research, most Selling Assistants without employees who are just starting out may want to register as either a Sole Proprietorship (if you are running the business alone) or a Partnership (if you have a business partner). The Sole Proprietorship is the least expensive business type to form, requires the least work and is also the least closely regulated, so it usually best fits the needs of an individual working from home. Another option is a Single Member Limited Liability Corporation (LLC) but this business type, while affording less liability, is more work and a greater expense to form, though it does provide more legal protection.

Keep in mind, this is just a very general overview as a starting point for your own research. Please do not consider this legal counsel. If you plan to hire an accountant or bookkeeper anyway to help with record keeping, you may want to consult with them before starting the registration process to make sure you're doing the right thing in your area and for your specific situation.

REGISTERING A BUSINESS NAME

Before we go any further, you should understand two things. Firstly, you can just use your legal name as the name of your business without having to do anything extra. This is the simplest option, involves the least amount of paperwork and may be the best choice when you're just starting out. With a Sole Proprietorship, this is even the default choice.

Secondly, while you can often register your business name at the same time as registering the business itself, it can also be a separate step if needed. For a fee, you can reserve a name for a business you aren't quite ready to start yet or know you'll need to change your business name at a later date. While this can mean an additional charge over registering your business and name at the same time, it can give you more freedom to either reserve a good name you're afraid someone else will steal or start a business under your own name and later change it to something else.

The biggest advantage to creating a unique business name for your service is that it makes it more memorable. It can also make your service seem more professional than just using your name. A clever choice can take some of the work out of marketing your service, helping you with word of mouth and letting customers know exactly what you do without their having to ask.

Believe it or not, you can't just make up any old name for your business and start using it. Prior to registering a name, you'll need to verify that it is available and not in use, a process your local registration office can walk you through. No matter how unintentional, it's very easy to step on someone else's copyright or trademark, and that can land you in expensive legal trouble. Do yourself a favor and register your business name, even if you're been using it informally for years without an issue. It's well worth the extra expense to know that you have the legal right to use the name of your choice, and that you won't lose it after building up a customer base.

Already have a registered business but want to separate out your Selling Assistance services? While you can register a second company, if the businesses are of a related nature, consider registering a "Trading As" or alternate name. That allows you to run your existing business under an alias for some projects, such as Selling Assistance services.

CHOOSING A BUSINESS NAME

Ultimately, what you call your business is up to you, but while this can seem like a simple step, there are a few things to consider before you commit to a name. The best business names have two things: memorability and branding.

A memorable name is one that will be easy for customers and clients to remember. This means your business name should be short and clever. You want something your customers will have no trouble calling to mind even if they have lost your business card. You also want a name unique enough that someone can easily find you through a simple internet search without being distracted by similar names.

Branding is the sum total of your company's public persona. A well-branded name should instantly give your customers a picture of what your company does and what it is like. Your brand is a complex subject, but it distills down to the identity of your company and how you present it to buyers.

Start to think about what your company will be like. What will you specialize in? How do you want to present yourself and your service? As silly as it may seem, visualize your company as a person. How would he or she talk, look and dress?

Start getting a picture in your head of how you want clients to see your service at first glance both from a visual and personality standpoint. The best branding starts with a feeling, so it's fine if you don't have any specifics at this point. But by at least taking a few minutes to think this out, you'll be more likely to know when you do find the right one.

Something else to consider: Many states allow you to

register a business name as long as it isn't in use in the state you're registering in. That means the name you choose may already be in use in another state. If your business is predominately local, this may not be an issue, but consider whether you can handle the competition of sharing a name, even with another company out of state. Another single-person company across the country with the exact same business name may not be a problem, but a large drop-off retail location just across the border could cause you issues in the long run. If possible, try to register your business on the national level. Yes, it's another additional expense, but the extra protection may be worth it in the online world.

Will your business name be related to your service itself or what you sell? "Action Figure Emporium" or "Priced Nostalgia" are examples of business names that relate only to the type of items the company sells. That name isn't trying to attract SA clients, only customers to buy the items once they are on sale. From the name alone, you have no idea if this company offers Selling Assistant services at all. A SA with a name that relates only to what they sell will need to do more marketing to secure clients, but a name that relates to your sales niche can mean a bigger customer base and greater sales volume, which increases the value of your SA service.

What about a name like "Morris County Consignments" or "Cash for Clutter"? Names like these wouldn't tell a buyer what sort of items you sell, but they would easily tell prospective SA clients what your company does at a glance. This is the ideal option for someone creating a separate name for their Selling Assistance services and can also work as the primary business name.

Can you create a business name that relates both to what you sell and the SA service you offer? If you can come up with one, that may be the perfect compromise. Another consideration is registering a "Trading As" or alternate name in addition to your business name. You could make the main business a name that relates to your SA service while the alternate name is the name that you actually sell the goods under. Alternately, if being a SA is only part of your larger business, then the alternate name might be a better fit for only that offshoot service.

Are there advantages to registering your selling and Selling Assistance as two completely different companies? That's a question for your accountant. The answer may change as your business grows.

While I can't tell you exactly how to pick a name that will fit your specific business, here are some general tips for you to consider that I hope will guide you through this process.

- **Make sure you're spelling the name of your business correctly and that it is grammatically correct.** Maybe you're intentionally being creative with spelling or phraseology to be clever, but you'd be amazed at how many people register a business name with simple errors unintentionally. You can't possibly check this enough times before finalizing.

- **How does your chosen name compare to what's already out there?** Before you register anything, do a variety of searches for the prospective name online. If you Google the name and discover half a dozen similar names that are all too easy to confuse with yours, it's time to rethink your choice.

- **Say the business name out loud.** Try it in different regional accents if possible. Something that sounds slick and professional in your native tongue can sound like a sex position in another part of the country.

- **Type the business name as it would look as a username, url or hashtag, i.e. all as one word without capitals or punctuation.** Your domain name, user ID on sites like eBay or Etsy and social networking handles will usually be this form of your company name. Pen Island seems like a great name for your stationary store until you realize that without the space it becomes "penisland."

- **Is the name you're considering available as a domain**

name (i.e. a custom URL web address ending such as a **.com or .net)?** Discovering after you've already registered your business name that someone else is using the matching url isn't the end of the world, but it can be both annoying and expensive to secure a domain from the another owner, assuming they're even willing to give it up. Otherwise, you're looking at registering an alternate version of your business name that may not match what you registered, causing client and customer confusion. It's free to check on the availability of any url so it's better to do so before you're committed to a name.

- **Make sure you're not stepping on anyone's copyright or trademark, even if you're trying to be cute.** For instance, your name is Sally Star and so you decide to call your SA service "Star Bucks." Parody laws only go so far, and as soon as you start making profit under a name like that, even if it's a completely different type of business, you're going to find yourself in trouble. It's not worth it. Your tiny little company cannot survive being sued by one of the big guys. Save yourself the trouble and steer clear of anything someone else owns.

- **Be careful with puns.** They can make for clever business names but have their own set of pitfalls. I'm always complimented on how clever the name of my blog, TheWhineSeller.com, is, but while it works when written out, it doesn't when spoken. When I meet connections in person or do podcast or radio appearances, I always have to spell the name or people mix up the homophones when they try to find me later. In the same way, if a pun or alternate spelling is all that separates your business name from another, you may unintentionally send traffic to your competitor. If they are running a similar service, they could easily take your confused customers.

- **Your business name is every customer or client's first impression of you.** You may think a name like "eBitch" or "Psycho Seller" is funny or ironic, but it can turn buyers or potential clients off. Whimsy and clever are both great features for a name, but you still want a measure of professionalism.

If you're having trouble coming up with a name, start brainstorming. Write down any and all words that you associate with your service and that feel you had for what your finished business brand will be like. Force yourself to fill a whole sheet of paper, no matter how silly some of the options feel. Once they're all together visually, combinations and possibilities should start to become apparent. Start a second list of the combinations that jump out and whittle it down to the final name from there. If you really get stuck, consult a rhyming dictionary or thesaurus for additional inspiration.

A very simple litmus test for your business name is to ask friends, family or, best yet, acquaintances who don't necessarily like you all that much, what they think of it. After taking so much time to come up with a name (or names if you haven't narrowed it down yet), you really need the opinion of someone with some distance from it. Sometimes a person on the outside can see the missing piece from their fresh perspective.

CLAIMING YOUR BUSINESS NAME ONCE IT'S YOURS

Once you've settled on a business name, taken the steps to ensure your name is available for use and registered it, you'll want to take the time to protect that name. It may seem like a silly step now when no one's even heard of your business yet, but taking a few minutes to protect your name now will save you headaches in the future.

As soon as your business name is rightfully yours, you should strongly consider taking some of the following steps:

Register a domain name a.k.a. a custom URL web address such as "YourCompanyName.com." I was intimidated by domain names for years. To my surprise, when I finally looked into buying my own, I discovered that it's not only extremely easy to register for one, they are also quite inexpensive. You can register a domain, in many cases, for half the cost of a cup of coffee, and the process takes minutes.

The advantages to having your own domain name are many, even if you only use it to point to your store or listing page on a platform like eBay and don't have an external website. For one, it's an easy way to direct buyers to your website, particularly if your domain matches your company name. Buying your domain also ensures that someone else, be they a competitor or a completely different company, can't register it themselves and confuse your customers.

Should you also buy similar domain names to yours just in case? For example, buying your domain as a .net in addition to .com or buying alternate spellings? I personally don't believe that it's essential, but if the price is right, it can be a good investment you may choose to make to ensure no one else can grab them out from under you.

Set up a designated email address for your SA service. While you could use a free email service like Gmail, Hotmail, AOL or Yahoo, it looks far more professional to use an email address on your new custom domain. You can even set that email up with POP or IMAP through almost any free email service or program if you're more comfortable with that interface. Luckily, almost all domain name purchases include at least a few email addresses at your new domain (and many include an unlimited number), so you probably gained this new address when you registered your web address at no additional charge. The other added bonus to an email at your new domain is that every message you send or receive automatically advertises your business.

Whether free or on your custom domain, having a separate email address for your business, especially for your SA service, can minimize mistakes.

Register your business name on the main social networks. Once the name you've chosen is registered and officially yours, start claiming it wherever possible. While there is a charge for registering a domain name or URL, signing up your new business name for things like a Facebook page, Twitter account, Google+ page, or Tumblr blog are all free. Even if you aren't ready or even sure that you'll ever use a service or social network, it's well worth it to take the minute it takes to sign up just in case.

Not only will this ensure that you've got your name waiting for you if you later decide to use that tool or service, but it also prevents someone else from snagging the name out from under you. Better to have an account that you never use than to discover that someone else is using your name in a way that damages your reputation and causes customer confusion. Reserving your business name and username on any of these sites only takes a few minutes and can save you many headaches down the road.

MERGING YOUR NEW BUSINESS NAME WITH YOUR SELLING IDENTITY

In the same vein, because this business will be so closely affiliated with your selling activity, now's the time to reconsider the name you sell under. If you're using the same business name for both your Selling Assistance services and your actual selling space, it's a good idea to make sure you'll be able to secure a storefront or username that's as similar as possible to your business name. If you've sold in the past under something informal, consider changing it to something that better reflects your new professional status. Selling Assistance clients will look at your store when considering your services even if you're using a separate name so you want to make sure you're showing them your best side.

While you have the option of changing your user ID or username on sites like eBay or Etsy for no charge at any time with minimal restrictions, the more often you change it, the more you run the risk of losing the relationships you've built up on that platform. Once you find the best name for your service, set it and stick with it. That said, if you've recently had some bad press or other negative experiences and you feel that your business name is soiled, you may wish to change your name to disassociate yourself with that bad experience.

There are restrictions on what most marketplaces allow as part of a username, and you may not be able to use your business name exactly as registered. It might be worth it to let these restrictions inform your business name selection process at the start or just commit to creating an abbreviated or modified version of your registered name as a User ID.

SHOULD I REGISTER A SEPARATE SELLING ACCOUNT?

If you already have an established selling identity, you've got to decide whether you'll be selling your clients items through that account or if you'll create a separate account just for SA items. The account that you use for your Selling Assistance service is likely to have a high volume of transactions and thus will benefit from volume seller discounts and advantages (such as eBay's PowerSeller or Top Rated programs, which offer discounts, advanced search placement, etc.), increased feedback numbers and buyer traffic. All of these will benefit all your listings, whether they are your items or those of your clients, so it can be advantageous to keep all you selling activity on one account. Knowing their items will be in a thriving storefront can be a big selling point that encourages a prospective client to entrust you with their items.

However, particularly as your business grows, you may want to have separate accounts for several reasons. Firstly, a single account makes accounting complicated as you'll need to keep your inventory separate from what you're selling for clients. If you stock and consign similar items, it can quickly get confusing. Secondly, it may behoove you to have a separate selling account for each of your niches to keep each specialty in its own sales space. Lastly, if your personal inventory has a strong theme or focus, separating out the consignment items can ensure that you don't dilute your main selling brand with irrelevant items. This would give you more freedom to take SA items you wouldn't normally, as you don't have to worry about their being in your personal store.

REGISTRATION REDUX

Let's review the incredibly important steps of getting your business registered and your name reserved.

- Register your business with your local or national government for additional financial protection for both you and your company.

- Register a name for your business to officially preserve it for your use.

- Choose a name for your business that is both memorable and tied to your brand identity.

- Take the time to reserve your business name on social networks or with a custom URL or email address to ensure that no one else steals your business identity online.

- Determine how your Selling Assistant services will relate to your existing selling identity and merge or separate accordingly.

RECORD KEEPING

The biggest thing that seems to turn people off to the idea of having a registered business is record keeping. Keeping careful records is very important regardless of whether you're keeping them to hand to an accountant or use yourself, and they are your best defense in the event of an audit or lawsuit. You'll need to keep track of all expenses, income, clients, their payments, marketplace selling and payment processing fees, item sales, marketing costs and much more. I know many experienced sellers that are driven to tears by the very thought of doing their own expenses, but you shouldn't let this part intimidate you because it's really not as bad as it seems.

Exactly what kind of records should you keep for your

business? You'll need to document all the money that goes in and out in detail and keep everything about your financial state as transparent as possible. At the most basic, it's a record of the classic Who, What, When, Where, Why and How you learned about in school.

- **WHO did you receive money from or pay money out to?** In this case, this refers not just to individuals such as clients but also companies. Say X dollars in fees went to Etsy, Y dollars went to Staples for the purchase of that new desk, and Z dollars came in from the Amazon Associates referral program you use to promote your items. You'll need a record of everyone, including companies, you do business with.

- **WHAT money went in and out?** This is your individual expense and income transactions.

- **WHEN did each transaction happen?** Here's where "I bought that printer sometime in March" isn't good enough. Your credit card or bank statement is your best friend for giving you the exact dates for every payment and purchase you make.

- **WHERE did the money go?** I like to think of this as the "See? I'm not embezzling!" one. Keep a paper trail of where the money you earn went both in terms of where you store it, such as a bank account, and where it was spent.

- **WHY did you spend or pay out that money?** A few basic expense and income categories to get your started might be Shipping Costs, Marketplace Fees, Marketing Costs or Client Payments. You'll discover the need to add more as you go, but the idea is to organize your earning and spending into simple categories.

- **HOW did the money travel?** Was it a credit card payment? Check? With which bank? You'll need to know how each transaction came and went.

Seems like a lot written out like that, doesn't it? But most of the time you can get the answers to all five of these questions in a single line item. For instance, if I write that I paid $5 to FedEx on January 14, 2014 for the shipment of John Doe's item via my American Express credit card, the WHO is John Doe, the WHAT is $5, the WHEN is January 14th, the WHERE is to FedEx, the WHY is the expense category Shipping Costs, and the HOW is my American Express credit card.

See? Not really all that complicated after all. The five questions are just a simple memory tool to help you make sure you've got all the details. It really just comes down to keeping a record of all the little specifics behind every transaction.

For most of us, nearly all the info we need will come from a couple of places: the marketplace we sell in will give us the info about individual transactions, our credit card statement will keep a record of every expense, and our payment processor, such as a PayPal account or similar, will be a record of all of our income. Of course, your business may also have a checking account, use several payment processors or accept cash payments, but you get the idea. Your job is just to take this info and organize it in a meaningful way.

KEEPING AN EYE ON THE BOTTOM LINE

Whether you hire someone to take care of your finances for you or opt to do your own bookkeeping, I still recommend combing through your records regularly yourself, particularly in the beginning when your business is new. It's easy to get caught up in the day-to-day selling and lose sight of the big picture. You'll want to check the numbers monthly and adjust your services accordingly.

Look at your expenses versus income at the end of each month. There are a few simple questions to ask yourself to give you an idea of what you're looking for. Namely…

- **Are you actually making money?** Before you roll your eyes at this one, you'd be amazed at how many people, particularly online sellers, get so wrapped up in the process of selling that they never realize they're actually losing money or only breaking even. Don't just assume you're making a profit, look at the numbers regularly and make sure you know exactly how much money your business is bringing in over sending out.

- **Where does the money come from?** Not everything you do in a day to run your business will directly result in income, but you'll want to keep in mind which aspects of your business do. This way you'll remember to give them the bulk of your focus instead of getting distracted by necessary, but not as profitable, activities such as social networking. It's simple. The more of the profitable activities you do, the more money you'll make.

- **Where does the money go?** Expenses are necessary to running a business but the less overhead you have, the more profit you'll make. Always look for ways to trim your budget down and eliminate unnecessary expenditures whenever possible.

- **How does the money you're making compare to how much work you're doing?** Keep track, even a rough estimate, of your working hours over the course of the month. Say you discover that you're making $200 a week from your Selling Assistance business. If you're only spending 8 hours a week working on it, you're making $25 an hour, so that's pretty darn good. But if you're working 40 or more hours a week to earn that $200, you need to rethink things. Your time is probably worth more than that.

If your work-to-profits balance is off, take a look at your biggest expenses and profits. At the most basic, you can increase your profits by decreasing your expenses. What expenses can you trim to give yourself more in the bottom line?

As for profits, look at the activities that result in the most profit. How can you do them faster or more efficiently? Now look at the activities that result in the least amount of profit. Are you wasting a lot of time on stuff that doesn't translate into income? Can you cut out or outsource some of those activities to free you up to spend more time on the more profitable elements of your business? If you can keep at least the same amount of income but decrease the number of hours you work, that will not only increase how much you make per hour but also free up more of your time to get more high-paying work done.

Staying on top of your records can help you adapt your business to make it the best it can be and to catch issues before it's too late. If you only look at your finances once a year, at tax time, you may end up with a nasty surprise when there's no time left to make any adjustments and save your bottom line. Keeping a regular eye on the numbers will give you a better understanding of how it works and how to make it work even better.

But keep this in mind whenever you look at your finances: The government expects it to take a new business a maximum of three years to start turning a profit before it must be downgraded to a hobby. If you aren't turning a profit or if you're only turning a small profit in the beginning, don't panic. It takes time to build up any new business, and your first year will be filled with set-up expenses that you won't have again the next year. As long as there is growth, no matter how slow, that's a good sign.

DOING IT YOURSELF

I've been doing my business finances myself for years, and I swear to you, it's really not that bad. It's one of those things that seems more intimidating than it really is, and the first time you do it is really the worst time. Once you've got a system in place, you'll only be doing some quick data entry once a quarter or so.

While I have an accountant that files our business taxes once a year, I do all my company finances myself in Quickbooks. Popular accounting software like Quickbooks, Quicken or Peachtree can be expensive and may be a bit more than you need unless your business, like mine, has several elements to it beyond the your Selling Assistance service. There are many financial software options available that are cheaper and simpler than the bestsellers. For that matter, even a simple spreadsheet can be used for keeping records such as Microsoft Office Excel or Google Sheets.

A good free option that's a little more advanced is Money Plus Sunset Deluxe (formerly Microsoft Money). A desktop program from Microsoft, it's pretty simple to use with most of the features you'll need. I actually used Money exclusively for many years before I switched to Quickbooks when my business grew.

Accounting software is very popular right now and a quick internet search should give you dozens of options. There are even a few under the third party application section in eBay itself. While looking for the best option for your business, consider focusing on time-saving features like automatic import from the marketplaces and payment processors you use the most often, convenience factors like mobile accessibility and cloud back-ups and, most importantly, privacy and safety of your data.

Doing your finances yourself saves you the cost of hiring someone to do it, but it may also mean you're more likely to make costly mistakes without someone double-checking you. You'll have a closer eye on your finances so you'll catch issues earlier than someone who's outsourcing it, but it also means more work. Which is the right way to go? That will depend on how you feel about diving into the numbers and minutiae of your business or whether you'd rather leave that to someone else.

The biggest reason I would suggest doing your own finances? No one knows your business better than you.

HIRING A BOOKKEEPER OR ACCOUNTANT

But maybe you just aren't comfortable working with numbers and records or maybe your business is too large or complex for you to effectively manage your records yourself.

Perhaps it's time to consider hiring someone to help with the company finances. But do you need an accountant or bookkeeper? Or both?

What's the difference? Some people use the terms interchangeably, and you'll see accountants that offer bookkeeping services and vice versa. At their most basic, a bookkeeper mostly does data entry while an accountant focuses more on analysis, guidance and advice on the data someone else has already organized. You may need one of each or you may find someone who offers both types of service in tandem.

What do you feel you need the most help on? If you're perfectly happy to do the data entry but really need a good financial mind to look at the numbers and guide you, that's very different from someone who knows exactly how their business is heading and what to do but just doesn't feel like doing the boring part of plugging in numbers. Are you looking for something where you just hand everything over in a disorganized mess, and they magically make it all neat, or are you willing to do some organization before passing it along to the professional?

Start to consider your needs before you look for someone to hire. There's no point in paying for services you won't need or hiring someone who only does part of what you want. Once you have a clear idea of what you're looking to have done, you'll find it that much easier to narrow down who'd be the most help.

When it comes to your money, you can never be too careful, so a personal recommendation or a well regarded local person would be ideal. Here's one case where I would recommend going local over online for the simple reason that there is a level of trust you can expect from someone who's a part of your same community and has a neighborhood reputation to maintain over someone on the other side of the world. If you already have an accountant that does your taxes, see if she or he can offer a referral. Failing that, ask around at other local businesses and see if they'll tell you who they use.

Choosing to pay someone to do your bookkeeping over doing it yourself is an extra cost that can cut into your profits, but anything you pay out to a bookkeeper or accountant is a business expense and therefore tax deductible. Hiring someone to take over the financial stuff may free you up to do other important work that results in more income anyway. A professional accountant may also provide an extra layer of protection, offering support in the event of an audit and acting as a second pair of eyes to look over your data and catch mistakes.

AUCTIONEER LAWS

One of the big reasons eBay no longer runs their official Selling Assistance program is because they kept running afoul of auctioneering laws and weren't equipped to help sellers navigate them. While there is no federal law in the US governing auctions, each state has different requirements for running auctions, and by running an SA service, you'll need to make sure you're in compliance. This could mean an additional license, fees or taking certain classes. While not every state's laws will affect your service, you'll want to read up on what applies where you'll be doing business and make sure that you're running everything in a way that won't land you in trouble.

GETTING IT IN WRITING: CONTRACTS AND AGREEMENTS

The term "contract" can sound pretty frightening, but in the end, all it amounts to is a written record of the terms of the agreement between the Selling Assistant and the client. Having a written agreement protects both of you: it protects the client if the SA does not fill the terms as promised and also protects the SA if the client violates those same terms. While nearly all your transactions will go smoothly, you don't want to leave yourself unprotected in the event of a problem. No matter who you're doing business with, whether they be a family member, close friend or consistent client, make sure they have an agreement and contract signed before each new batch of items. Get everything in writing. Even if it seems like overkill, it could save your business if there's an issue and you end up in court.

Please note that all of the information provided in this section is no substitute for the advice of an attorney and are only suggestions. I am not a legal professional and am not licensed to give out legal advice. The money you spend on an attorney to draft you a contract template that you can use for all future sales is well worth the money if it saves you from legal problems down the road.

You should have a signed contract before either you (on a pick-up) or they (for a drop-off) drive away with the items. If you plan to leave the items at the client's location, make sure the contract is in place before you list the items. It's a good idea to email your client a copy of the contract ahead of time so you won't have to wait while they go over it.

For a fee, you can have the contract signatures notarized. In this case, a certified notary public witnesses your signature and validates it with an official seal for a fee. You may be surprised to find that many copy and printing stores are also notaries public. Having both signatures notarized provides you with extra protection, but it's an extra expense and hassle you may not want to deal with.

Unless you will have access to a copy machine at the signing, it's best to bring two copies of the contract and just have both parties sign twice. This way you can be certain that both you and the client have a copy on file. Electronic copies of the signed contract are fine too if you've got an easy way to send one.

Make sure that the current contact info of both parties is on the contract including mailing address, email address, and at least two phone numbers. Not only will this be a helpful resource for you to refer back to, it also ensures that if there's a breakdown in communication, you're in the clear as long as you stuck to the contact methods they gave you.

The simplest way to create a SA/Client contract is to modify the list of policies, features, and upgrades that we created in the previous section into more professional language. Then add a statement that both parties agree to the terms written above and add a place for both you and your client to include your contact info. Feel free to combine several elements in one item.

Here's a very basic example. This is my base template
for eBay Selling Assistance, the one I build all my other contracts
up from, so it only has my most rudimentary terms on it and
doesn't include any of my extended features like pick-ups. This
text is provided as a sample only and should not be considered

PRICED NOSTALGIA SELLING ASSISTANT AGREEMENT

This agreement is made on _____ between Priced Nostalgia, herein referred to
as "Selling Assistant", and _____ herein referred to as "Client."
Whereas Client wishes for the Selling Assistant to sell the items listed on the
attached sheet by consigning said item(s) to the Selling Assistant for sale on
eBay, it is understood:

- That Selling Assistant will make every attempt to obtain the best
  possible price for the consigned merchandise and where the Client has
  indicated a minimum price will accept no less than that value.

- That for her efforts Selling Assistant is entitled to retain 20% of the final
  sale price.

- That, should a sale be effectuated, Selling Assistant shall forward a check
  for the amount of the full purchase price, less the aforementioned percentage
  and less any eBay or PayPal fees incurred on the sale, to Client within 30
  days of payment clearance.

- That a payment is considered cleared when either eBay's 60 day return window
  has passed or the buyer leaves positive feedback, whichever comes first.

- That Selling Assistant represents that she maintains insurance for theft and
  damage, and that the consigned merchandise will be covered by said insurance
  while it is in her possession.

- That Client agrees to leave the merchandise with Selling Assistant for a
  minimum of 90 days.

- That should the merchandise remain unsold at the end of the
  consignment period and an election be made by the Client
  to remove said merchandise, any costs incurred by the delivery
  of same to Client shall be borne by Client.

Selling Assistant   Client

Name: _____   Name: _____

Phone #: _____   Phone #: _____

Alt Phone #: _____   Alt Phone #: _____

Email: _____   Email: _____

Signed: _____   Signed: _____

legal for use as is. It should, however, at least give you an idea of
how to get started.

REVIEW

It can be easy to get so caught up in the flurry of actually running your business that you forget to keep track of everything. Your records are what will help shape the future of your company and protect you legally, so they're too important to ignore. Let's take a moment to review the main things to remember when it comes to keeping your business current by recording the past.

- Keep your business protected and balanced by carefully recording of the Who, What, When, Where, Why and How of every transaction.

- Watch your income, expenses and working hours vigilantly to ensure that your business is actually making money proportional to what you're putting into it and adjust accordingly.

- Consider doing your finances yourself to save money and keep a closer eye on where you business is heading.

- Consider hiring a bookkeeper or accountant to handle your finances if the extra cost of having a professional do it outweighs the annoyances of doing it yourself.

- Make sure you're in compliance with in local auctioneer laws, which may involve taking classes or additional licenses or fees.

- Protect yourself and get everything in writing by having a contract that outlines all your terms and policies.

CLIENTS AND THEIR ITEMS

We've designed our service. We've registered our business and set up everything related to it. We're officially ready to start offering our services to people with something to sell.

So far, we've mostly talked about how a Selling Assistant service runs from the seller's end, but that really only gives you half the picture. A Selling Assistant spends the majority of their time working with clients and their items. While your business and terms are the bread, it's the items you have to sell that are the real meat of your service, and without clients, you're not making a profit.

Let's take some time to get to know the most important part of your Selling Assistant service.

CLIENT CONTACT: WHAT'S IT LIKE?

HELLO

What your first communication with a client will look like depends on both who contacted who and how. If you're the one reaching out to the client, you'll have the luxury of presenting everything in the best possible way to make your job easier. Might you have them fill out a form ahead of time? Will you have a pamphlet or other handout that explains your service in detail? You'll know best what you need to make a SA contract go smoothly so you'll have a sense of the best way to start off on the right foot.

If the client contacts you, it will usually be a single email or phone message where they just give their name, mention that they have items to sell, and give you their contact info to return their message. Occasionally, they will actually tell you what they've got to sell, but this is frustratingly rare so you'll just have to contact them back to get more information. The client usually won't be specific about what they want to hire you for upfront, and you'll need to extract the details yourself to get an idea of what to expect.

Because so many initial contacts are vague and you'll find yourself asking the same follow-up questions each time, I highly recommend composing a form email or a phone script to save yourself time. Taking a few minutes to write up a couple of stock answers for each of your most common scenarios is worthwhile since you'll not only never need to craft that message again, you'll also be sure you're always saying something professional and thought-out instead of whatever is on the top of your head. Just be aware that you'll probably need to tweak a sentence or two to tailor to specific situations.

Regardless of whether the client contacts you via email or telephone, if possible, call them back on the phone. Speaking to a person on the phone instills confidence because it puts a human voice to the service and also gives you a trust advantage over anyone who just emails back. If you do not catch the person when you call, do leave a message, but also send them an email message to make sure your bases are covered.

No matter who initiated contact, the first part of any client contact is to convince them to consider your SA service.

WHAT DO YOU HAVE FOR ME TO SELL?

Once you've initiated contact with a client, you need to get an understanding of what they have to offer. While you likely already know what your client has to sell if you're the person who sought them out, you'll still need additional details, and you'll usually have little to no info when the client's the one coming to you. This can mean that you meet, either via drop-off hours or scheduled pick-up, and take a look at what they have in person.

Personally, I don't like to make the trip out to meet with a client until I know their items are worth my time. That's why I require, upon first contact, that the client write up a detailed list of exactly what they have for me to sell. Some balk at the idea of doing any work, which is why I always point out that this list is for their protection so they have a list of exactly what they gave me to serve as a receipt. This list actually becomes part of our final client contact, so it's an important step that has to be done either way.

For this list to be useful, it requires as much detail as possible such as brand name, condition, any details they remember about the items' history and if they have a reserve price in mind. While their info will never be 100% accurate, it will at least give you a starting point when you do your own research into the item. The reserve price is particularly important because an item you won't be able to sell for as much as the client wants is no different from an item you wouldn't be able to sell at all.

That said, asking prospectives to do any work ahead of time can cost you clients. They may have had a momentary burst of inspiration to call you and tell you that they had "some stuff" to sell but actually telling you what that stuff is may be more work than they're willing to do, so they'll never follow up. After that initial chat via email or telephone, you request a list of what they have, and though they sound agreeable to the idea, you'll actually never hear from them again. This happens very frequently. To me, I see this as an acceptable trade off and a way to weed out the people I wouldn't want to be working with anyway.

If the client seems to have really good items and you're worried that asking them to write up the list makes them a flight risk, you may prefer to set up a time to meet and go over the items yourself. Location could be a big factor to this. If a client lives minutes from your door, it's less trouble to evaluate their items yourself than if it would take an hour roundtrip to look at items that are a complete unknown. If a client you were excited about disappears, don't be afraid to initiate follow-ups yourself. It's entirely possible they just forgot and may be still interested in your service.

Very often, you'll know from the start if their items are worth selling, so don't be surprised if you frequently find yourself firing off a kind rejection after the very first contact. Not everyone has something of value to sell. Whenever possible, do try to convert those rejected clients into an income stream in another way either by offering tutoring, encouraging them to refer a friend or getting them to agree to send you other items in the future.

CLIENT ACCEPTANCE OR REFUSAL

No matter how you decide to handle evaluating their items, the important take away is this: just because a client contacts you, that doesn't mean you're under any obligation to sell their items until you've signed the contract. You can, and should, be discerning about what items you take on. Never be afraid to walk away from a commission for any reason but particularly if the work won't be worth the potential earnings.

But while you may go into every contract with this

mindset, the client may not realize that you aren't required to take on every contract that comes your way, so you'll want to be delicate with how you handle the rejection. Many people take their items very personally and will be offended and defensive on their behalf if you aren't interested in them. Whenever possible, blame the market, not their items to soften the blow and increase the likelihood you'll still get their business or word of mouth in the future. For instance, instead of telling them that their pile of common McDonald's toys isn't worth anything, you may want to spin it as not a good fit to sell online because that particular market is saturated. Whenever possible, suggest alternatives for items you're passing on, be it a local consignment shop, another local SA that has a different specialty than you, or a charity that accepts donations.

AGREEMENT OF TERMS

Once you've decided that a client is worth taking on, you'll need to agree to the terms of your service. You'll present them with your contract, which should detail all the specifics of how you'll run your service. Most clients will review your standard contract, ask a few questions for clarification, and then sign without further issue.

Some will be a bigger challenge. Most often, the people battling you over some element of your terms simply don't really understand how that part of your service works and some additional explanation smoothes things right over. Some just want to haggle, fighting you over the smallest things, such as a single percentage point on your commission, just because they like feeling like they're getting a special deal. Others want to tell you exactly how your service will run and what the terms will be. ("I'll only pay you $1 an item, and you'll get everything sold in 3 days, and that's my final offer!")

You'll need to evaluate case by case whether it's worth it to revise your terms to cater to a prickly client or to walk away. If you're regularly getting static over the same parts of your contract, you'll want to reevaluate that line item. It may be worth it to build in an imaginary fee that you never actually charge, you just make a point of waiving for every client for some reason or another so they feel like they won a victory. That way you can offer a special deal without ever having to make less than you budgeted for.

If possible, avoid discussing terms until after you know what kind of items they have for you, particularly if you offer different terms for certain item types. Let them know that if they can give you a sense of what they have, you can decide which of the packages you offer is the best for their needs. In turn, talking numbers first can scare a client off. Your commission or fee will seem much more reasonable after they have a better sense of how much work you will be doing for them.

Once you come to an agreement, you'll actually wait to sign the contract until you've seen the items and they're physically in your possession.

ACQUISITION OF ITEMS

Now that you've agreed to the terms, the buyer either comes to drop their items off with you or you go to get them. You'll likely bring a copy of the contract you agreed upon for them to sign while you're there. I like to bring two to make sure they've got a copy as well.

A drop-off is usually a fairly simple exchange. Your client brings their items to you, you check them against what you were promised, you both sign the contract, and that's it. Just be sure to have a way to transport the items in the event that they brought them loose with no box or bag to carry them in.

Pick-ups, particularly at an individual's residence, can be a little more complicated. The best clients will have organized their items and have them packed up and ready for you to take as soon as you arrive. Many will not, however, and will either be handing you an item here, an item there or expect you to come into their house to get the boxes. Stipulate ahead of time some guidelines for pick-up. You may be willing to go into a client's foyer to help them carry boxes, but do you want to climb up into their attic and rummage around with them until they find the item they promised you?

When I was running my SA service as a teenager, I always required my clients have the items ready to go either in their entry way or outside the house, and I stipulated that I would not enter their residence. This was mostly a safety concern, as I was a young girl working alone and I didn't want to get into a bad situation. But even with this stipulation, many clients ignored it, and it can make for an awkward situation when they're telling you to come in and get the boxes from the attic and you're refusing. It comes down to this double standard where people are thinking: "Well, of course you wouldn't want to enter the house of some weirdo, but that wouldn't apply to MY house" because everyone thinks they're the only normal one so the rules shouldn't apply to them. They can view this refusal to give them this extra level of trust as insulting, and it's frustrating for you. As silly as it may seem, having a scapegoat, such as vague "insurance reasons" or "medical restrictions," can make the client more understanding and it won't seem so personal to them.

That said, I had one client I ended up working with for several years, and we used to sign contracts over tea and cookies at her kitchen table. Then we'd literally walk around her house and she'd point to random stuff and ask, "Could we sell that?" and if I thought we could, I'd just take it then and there and add it to our list. She wasn't organized enough to get a batch together, but I made thousands of dollars on her various contracts because I was willing to roll with her a la carte method. Your terms are a general guideline, but never be afraid of throwing them away if the situation warrants.

Always carry some folded boxes just in case because you'll need a way to transport the items. If you're worried about your car, some old blankets to protect it from dirty items aren't a bad idea either. Be dressed casually, you'll probably be moving dusty items, but neatly so you still look professional. Always arrive on time or early, giving the client a call when you're on the way whenever possible.

Most importantly, carefully go over all the items before you assume possession of them. You'll want to make sure that your client not only gave you the items they promised, in the condition promised, but also to make sure that you've got everything. It's a bit like that little sheet they have you fill out before you rent a car: you want to document everything with the owner present so you can't be blamed for any omissions or damage you didn't notice until you drove away.

LISTING THE ITEMS

In most cases, your client has minimal involvement in the actual listing of the items, but this doesn't put a pause in your interaction with them. You'll likely need to contact them with questions at some point because no matter how good everyone's notes are, things always come up. You'll also want to keep them informed along the way. How involved you keep the client is up to you, but, at the least, you should notify your clients when their items are listed because many like to see the completed listings or even watch the auctions.

When you do notify your clients that their listings are live, you can recommend that they share them with friends who might be interested in the items, but you may also want to tactfully remind them of shill bidding policies on sites like eBay. Well meaning clients have tried to force the price of their items up with creative bids from themselves or friends. Tactics like that are against marketplace policies and can get your selling account suspended, so you'll want to just make sure they realize it's not a harmless thing to do.

In theory, there should be a break in client contact until their items sell, and it's time to send them their payment. In practice, however, your clients will frequently hound you for details of their listings while they are ongoing. One thing that can help with this is to show them how to view completed listings so they can see themselves if anything sold, and to share their in-progress reconciliation sheet with them. The simplest way to do this is to use the free Google Sheets to create the document and share it with your client, giving them only the privilege to view, not to edit. This way, whenever you update their account, they'll be able to see whatever you did without your having to specifically contact them. Of course, this may be a bit more transparency than you're willing to give so you may need to find your own alternative that will keep your clients impatience at bay without meaning extra work for you.

One of the best cures for an impatient client is a partial payment, so whenever you can safely issue one without putting yourself at risk, do it.

PAYMENT

Whether you're sending your client's income in multiple small payments or doing one big payment at the end, you'll usually just be sending out a payment and sending your client's reconciliation sheet along with it. Whether you do this electronically or via snail mail is up to you, but it will rarely be in person unless you have unsold items that you need to return to the client. Once you've sent out their payment, your last contact with the client will want to plant the seeds for future business and word of mouth, so now is an ideal time to mention your referral bonus or other incentives for recommending you to their friends before you part ways.

ADDITIONAL ITEMS

Very often, what you're thinking of as the end of a contract has really just been a test or trial run to the client. It's not uncommon, once they've seen your service in action and are pleased with the result, for a client to give you additional items. Sometimes they'll wait until the first contract is over, but more times than not, they'll just arrange a second drop-off or pick-up with more items mid-contract. From a protection standpoint, you'll want to add an addendum to their existing paperwork to bring these new items into your existing deal.

From a practical angle, you'll need to decide whether to treat these new items as a whole new contract or to just add them to the existing batch. I usually keep the same reconciliation sheet over the lifetime of my relationship with a client and just add new listings on as they come unless there's a long lapse between contracts. No matter how you choose to handle it, you'll discover that your relationship with a client is rarely ever over for good, so you'll want to stay professional and attentive all the way through the process.

UNSOLD ITEMS

No matter how carefully you choose your items, there will always be those that either don't sell at all or don't sell for as much as your client wanted. What you'll do with these items is something your contract should cover up front. While your client may want items they have reserve prices on back, they may not be eager to see the others return. Once you're certain you cannot sell any unwanted items no matter the price, you may want to either dispose of or donate them. Whichever you do, just be sure you have the client's consent ahead of time to avoid issues later.

WHO ARE A SELLING ASSISTANT'S CLIENTS?

As with any business, the key to meeting the needs of your customers is first understanding who they are. Once you have a clear picture of who is looking to hire a Selling Assistant, then you can adjust your business to best meet their needs and better anticipate their concerns. Though there will always be the occasional exceptions, I believe all clients can fit into some combination of the following basic categories. Keep in mind that you may find yourself with different fees, terms and conditions for each type of client.

SMALL BUSINESSES AND CORPORATE CLIENTS

Corporate customers are the hardest type of client to

secure, but I'm including them first because they are the very best client to get. The corporate client is the Holy Grail for the Selling Assistant. They represent not only steady work and income but also the best opportunity for building your company into a regular full-time source of revenue. A partnership with a local business of any size can be very profitable for both sides.

Many companies already have a presence online or are actively working to build one. They may have even posted their need for Selling Assistance like any other job opportunity, though they may be calling it something very different, so you'll need to look closely. In this case, the job will often be a position in their office and may even be a full-time salaried position with benefits. If you'd you been looking forward to working from home and being self-employed, an opportunity like this may not appeal to you, but a position like this provides the best chance to parlay your selling experience into a steady career. You'd be doing the same sort of thing, selling items for someone else, you'd just be doing in on their terms, in their space. But what you'd sacrifice in freedom, you'd make up for with steady work and the stability of regular income over doing it solo. It would be a mistake to not keep an eye on local job postings or maybe even connect with a recruiter to stay abreast of any opportunities that arise just in case a great opening becomes available.

But a Selling Assistant's biggest opportunities are the businesses that may not have ever considered selling their goods and services online. There are many local small businesses or even local franchises of chain stores who would like to have their own web presence but may have never even heard of a Selling Assistant, let alone considered hiring one. If you can sign a client like that, it can mean both steady work and profits on your terms.

Take a moment and think of all the local small businesses you frequent or even just drive past regularly. Now go to your favorite search engine and see how many of them have websites. Even of those that do have websites, how many are actually using it to sell something and not just list their phone number and hours?

Don't just limit your search to retail locations selling physical items. Think of restaurants, nail salons, barber shops, etc. How many businesses that offer gift certificates for services, goods or food aren't selling them online? Tech-savvy brick and mortar storeowners are still in the minority, and while many are eager to build their customer base by expanding into e-commerce, they often have no idea of how to begin.

This is where the Selling Assistant comes in. The SA can approach local businesses and offer them the opportunity to sell their products, bringing their merchandise or services to an unprecedented number of new costumers without having to pay more than your fee or commission. You'll sell their items for them, and they'll get to expand their reach. Whether you offer to sell their items on a marketplace like eBay or Etsy or set them up their own custom-branded storefront is up to you, and you could even offer a variety of ready-made packages so they could have their pick. Even from the perspective of a business owner that already has an online presence but may be paying for their web hosting, email list, web marketing and e-commerce provider separately, simply paying you to handle all of it can be a very attractive offer. There's a reason you're called a Selling Assistant; you're here to assist even tech-savvy businesses with some of the work.

Many businesses are more than happy to part with a small share of their profits in exchange for your handling the work and order processing, especially if you're taking your fee out of profits they weren't making anyway until you came along. Gift certificates, special packages or unusual experiences can all make great Selling Assistant items in addition to tangible goods. While physical items will need to be shipped, services and other experiences require no shipping. Keep your mind firmly out of the box when proposing your services to local businesses.

Some other ideas to get you started:

- **Sell goods on behalf of local non-profits, schools, and churches through eBay MissionFish Giving**

Works as fundraisers. For the many non-profits that currently cannot accept physical item donations, this can be a lifesaver for them, as you can convert donated items to cash for their coffers.

- **Local theatres, hotels, restaurants and other venues can offer special packages to would-be travelers.** Create combination deals between local clients for web exclusive deals like dinner and a movie or a night at the theatre and a hotel room for the night.

- **Merge similar items from different local business into a single storefront that will be both a destination itself and draw for more clients.** For example, if you contract with a dozen local restaurants to sell their gift certificates online through your SA service, you could list them all together in one storefront. Not only can you advertise this storefront on its own as a great destination to support local eateries or for travelers coming into your area, the very existence of the storefront itself will, in turn, attract more businesses that want to be part of it and share in that exposure.

- **Even service-oriented businesses where the info needed can be exchanged via email can be sold online and the resulting product sent electronically.**

Of course, a client that doesn't even know you exist or what your service does is going to be hard to secure. You'll not only need to go to them, you'll also need to do a lot of explaining to get them to even consider your service, especially when you're just starting out. But while there may be rejections and literal doors shut in your face in the beginning, every client you do manage to sign makes it that much more likely that you'll get others who will be willing to give it a try once they've seen the success others have had with your service. Like any big fish, they're hard to land, but when you do, it can be well worth it. One good corporate client can generate enough income that you won't need many, if any, others.

How exactly your service will be arranged for each client is something you'll need to work out with each one. That's the beauty of the SA program; you can create the opportunities you want for yourself.

Do you actually ship the items or do you forward the orders to the store to fill? Do you take the item pictures or does the store provide them? Do you manage their listings entirely or just do it in the beginning and then turn it over to them, offering support as needed at a consultant's fee? Depending on the volume of items you'll be selling for them, you may even want to offer corporate clients different terms than individuals (such as a flat fee per every 10 items, monthly fees instead of per item charges or a reduced commission, etc.) since they will be bringing you steady profits.

In many cases, once you've finished the initial set-up, the corporate client will be even be less work than a typical client because they'll have a finite and often static inventory that you'll only need to list once but can sell for months to years. How long would it take you to list a gift certificate in three denominations? Minutes, right? Now imagine earning your fee or commission on the sales of those listings for months or even years all from those few minutes of work, and you'll start to see why corporate clients are well worth the extra effort.

CRAFTERS, FREELANCERS AND OTHER CREATORS

Similar to local businesses are their home-based equivalent: crafters, freelancers and other creators. There are already many people in your community running a hobby out of their home making crafts, stationary products, jewelry, etc. who have great items that they either never sell outside of family, friends and the local craft fair or don't sell at all. If only they had a way to sell their items online but still have more time to concentrate on doing what they do best: making arts, crafts or other items!

Similarly, there are freelancers of all sorts in your area offering a variety of services ranging from things like writing, graphic or web design, music composition, etc. that could increase their business if they only widened their reach. That's where you come in. Even a tech-savvy freelancer may not have the time or inclination to start selling their services online or to broaden into additional marketplaces but may be willing to let you handle it for your usual fee or commission. Dealing with creative work that is predominantly digital such as design or writing projects makes your job even easier because there's nothing to ship.

What creators in your area could you approach? Would the local author like to sell autographed copies outside of book signings? Is there a painter in town who'd like greater exposure for their work? The guy who plays at your bar every Thursday has CDs for sale, but does he also sell them on his website?

Freelancers, crafters and other creators with something to sell are all excellent clients to secure because they'll have a steady of supply of items for you instead of a single batch. They can represent a reliable source of income that you can depend on between your other SA contracts. They can also be some of the easiest items to list. Once you set up a listing for their art, service, book or other items, you'll just need to manage the sales as they come in and shouldn't need to touch the listing itself unless they send you new items.

There is one concern you should be mindful of, though, and that's the dangers of selling an item that doesn't exist yet. If selling a service, craft or art commission where your client is creating the work based on the terms of the sale, just make sure that you, the seller, are protected in the event of issues such as non-delivery. This can be a case where it's better to sell through the client's account so that any penalties for failing to meet buyer expectations or item delivery schedule don't reflect poorly back on you. Just develop a plan on how you'll handle these issues so that problems won't catch you unawares when they happen.

INDIVIDUALS AND FAMILIES

The majority of a Selling Assistant's clients will be individuals and families. Unlike a corporate client that has a steady supply of similar items, most customers have a single batch of items that they want you to sell for them and then they are done. Typical Selling Assistant items from this group include home goods, toys, collectibles, antiques, and other items that your clients may have in their attic or garage.

Clients of this sort usually contact a Selling Assistant when they are downsizing, moving, or doing a big cleaning project and looking to make some room. It's also not uncommon to have a client contact you to help sell items from a deceased friend or relative or items their children have outgrown. A client looking to free up space is preferable to those looking to make some quick cash because they are more interested in getting rid of the items and are happy with whatever you can get for them. The client looking for cash will almost always be disappointed in what their items actually sell for, no matter how much that is.

The items that individuals and families will present you will usually be their personal items, often used. Everything about a contract with a family or individual will be much more informal than your relationship with something like a freelancer or business. But while you may have to learn to deal with the client who conducts your meeting in his boxers or having to step around the litter box when you come to pick up their items, you want to make sure that you always conduct yourself professionally and adhere to your terms to the best of your ability. You'll always want to present your service in the best possible light for your best chance at good word of mouth and future business.

One advantage to this informality is that it also results in more humanity and makes these contract that much more pleasant. While this can also mean additional annoyances with a difficult personality, in most cases, people are friendly and that makes everything feel less like work and more like a favor you're doing for a person you like. When issues do arise, people are also more understanding face to face, and that can make even a prickly situation go more smoothly.

While some clients will offer you a box of truly random items, many have a theme to their batch. Collectors especially will contact a Selling Assistant when they're looking to either downsize their collection or at least trim out some of their least favorite pieces. Collectors are great for three reasons. Firstly, their items are easier to list because you can usually use the same research and listing template for all of their items since they're part of a similar theme or set. Secondly, a collector is usually more knowledgeable about their items and more organized, giving you less cleaning and research work to do before listing, especially if their items are all mint-in-box. Thirdly, collectors usually collect more than one thing or may decide to downgrade even more later, so if you do a good job with their first batch, there can be more work in store.

CLIENT TYPES

Over my many years of running this service, I have noticed that the clients themselves typically fall into the following personality types. Since understanding your client is the key to giving them the best service, I wanted to outline these types in detail. Please understand that this section includes some sweeping generalizations to help you understand the most common personality types that you are most likely to encounter over the course of running this business. I understand that there are exceptions to every rule, and I'm using these for illustration purposes only.

THE TECHNOLOGY-CHALLENGED

Who are they? Members of this group may either never have touched a computer or they are limited in their computer skills to checking Facebook, email and other simple tasks. While a great many seniors and middle-aged adults have mastered the computer, the majority of this age group falls into this category, as they didn't grow up with computers as the present generation has. That said, you'd be surprised at how many young people, though they spend every waking second on their smartphones and tablets, have little understanding of the basic computing skills needed to sell online.

No matter their age, the people in this group have little to no desire, time or inclination to learn how to sell their items online.

Pluses

- **Low-Maintenance Customers.** Clients of this group are usually more "hands-off." They would prefer to hand their items to you, never see them again, and just receive a check in return. This also means that they are less likely to second-guess your work, question your actions, criticize your pictures and nitpick every word you put in the description as it is unlikely they will ever even bother to look at the listing. For them, your service happens offstage. They just want the check at the end and are not interested in the process that yielded that money.

- **High-Value Items.** This group often has the most valuable items to sell because they never tried to sell them themselves. The best of their collection is usually still there for you to profit from.

- **Quantity**. Older clients in particular have had an entire lifetime to accumulate stuff, which means that some of these clients have enough items to keep you busy for months to years. One client with a large quantity of items is often easier and more profitable than many clients with only a few items each.

- **Large Market.** This is, quite possibly, the largest market for SA work, as few in this demographic are likely to consider listing their items themselves and most would prefer to hire a SA to do the work. As computers take even a stronger hold in our society, however, and sites like eBay simplify the listing process to court this very group, this crowd shrinks a little bit with each year. But as the skills needed to be a successful seller aren't those the same as being a master at Candy Crush, the rise of technology doesn't mean there won't still be tech-challenged people looking to hire a SA.

Minuses

- **Hard to Reach.** This group is the hardest to market your services to because they aren't online. What good is advertising on social networks or through search engines if your target demographic isn't on those sites? Those that haven't chosen to familiarize themselves with technology are also the least likely to think of it as a solution to their problems so they're less likely to seek you out. It will take some extra legwork for you to find them.

- **Distrust of your service.** Everyone has a natural distrust of the unknown. Many technology-challenged people are distrustful of the computer in general, not to mention the internet and buying and selling online. They may also be distrustful of a service they don't completely understand. The best way to counter this distrust is by explaining your service in very clear and simple terms so they can see that you're being upfront about all of the details. Meeting you face to face or at least talking to you on the phone can help seal the deal.

THE TOO-BUSYS

Who are they? Busy career people, parents, and people with large quantities of items. This group may have sold an item or two themselves in the past and may even be an experienced seller, but they simply do not have the time or the desire to list the items they have to sell. Time is very valuable to this group, so your commission seems like a worthwhile trade for their time.

Pluses

- **Profitable**. The Too-Busys often have large quantities of items, and a larger quantity usually ensures higher profits. Many of the members of this group are also in the middle to upper class, so there is often a higher quality of items to sell.

- **Networking**. This group is a fantastic resource for referrals, as they often associate with many other people who are just as busy and would be eager to use your services if it worked out well for their friend.

Minuses

- **Micromanaging.** Since they are computer savvy and may even have experience with selling, the Too-Busys are more likely to keep a close eye on your listings and to second-guess your work. I have found that busy people, particularly those in executive or other management roles in an office setting, want to have constant and very direct control over you and your work as if they were your boss. This can be very irritating if you're used to working independently and frustrating when they question how you do things. It may seem odd that a Too-Busy would hire you to do something for them only to micromanage and question your every move, but most busy people are at least part workaholic or control freak, and I include myself in that. It comes part and parcel with working as much as they do, so there isn't anything you can do to avoid it other than to make sure to have very good justifications, data, and examples to back up the decisions that you make and that you've developed a professional way of telling them to back off.

- **Always in a rush.** Their lives move at a breakneck pace, so at times, the Too-Busys have trouble understanding that the world of e-commerce sometimes involves a lot of waiting. This group is the least patient. Make sure these clients are clear from the start that even though an auction may only take a week, they need to take into account the full amount of time involved in listing the auction, waiting for payment, shipping the item, dealing with returns, etc. before you can send their payment.

- **Need it Yesterday.** Too-Busys also often have an unrealistic concept of time. You tell them the check will go out in 2 weeks, and 48 hours later, they want to know why it hasn't arrived yet. The best way to combat this impatience is have excellent, regular communication and to make your payment terms and time period very clear in the contract, and make sure that they not only sign it but keep a copy for their reference. If you know the exact day the auctions will be listed and you can give them an exact date when they will get payment, that would be ideal. The more you can keep them in the loop, the less they'll worry. However, if you do provide an exact date, be sure to leave yourself enough room to be able to collect from the buyers and deal with any issues before you have to turn the funds over. In general, try to keep the lines of communication open so they'll never feel like you've forgotten about them.

YOU'RE THE PRO

Who are they? This group has either never tried to sell online or done it only a few times, but unlike the Technology-Challenged, they have a strong desire to learn. In fact, this desire to learn is the biggest problem with this group. They intend to use you to list a few items for them while they learn the process from you. This group is saving their best items to sell themselves once they learn eBay, and they intend to learn eBay from watching you sell an item or two.

The best way to get a feel for any client is to start chatting with them about their items and their interests. If you notice that the person is only offering you a handful of items but eluding to many more items that he or she does not offer to let you sell or mentioning how long they have wanted to learn about selling online themselves, warning bells should go off in your head. If the items are good and you think you can still make a good profit on them, go for it, just make sure you don't let yourself be used for free lessons.

Pluses

- **Potential for Change.** "You're the Pros" can often turn into Too-Busys once they see how much work being an online seller really is. By doing a good job of selling their items, they may come back to you with the rest of their items once they decide that your commission is worth not having to do the work.

- **Ideal for tutoring.** If you're offering an element of selling education as part of your service, clients like these are a great opportunity. There's the potential to profit from the sale of their items through your SA service and also by offering lessons to show them how to sell for themselves in the future. They may balk at the idea of paying for knowledge they were hoping to get for free, but they may also go for it, giving you another revenue stream. And if they later decide that it's too much work to sell the items themselves, well, they know where to find you.

Minuses

- **Stingy with the Items.** You're the Pros will usually only give you a few items that are unlikely to sell at all or sell for very little, leaving you with very little profit for your efforts. They usually hold back their best items to sell themselves once they've learned from watching you.

- **Time Suckers.** Clients like this plan to use you to teach them how to sell online, so they can take up a lot of your time with questions about how the process works and requests for you explaining the basics, taking your time away from making money on other clients. There's a fine line between keeping them happy and making it clear that you're not there to be their teacher… unless they're willing to pay you for that.

You don't want to avoid clients like this entirely, but don't be afraid to say no if you meet one that's more trouble than they're worth. They're still a good source of referrals and potential income even if they have an ulterior motive. Even the most annoying client may come back with more items, and often of a higher quality, in the future, and you may not mind the free lessons if they're a good enough customer. Just be aware of how much of your time any single client dominates for how much profit they generate. You may be perfectly willing to answer questions for an hour with that client that makes you thousands of dollars a week, but you should stop yourself before giving that much time to that client with that one $20 item unless you can work it to your advantage.

THE GARAGE SALER

Who are they? The Garage Saler is the client who has heard that one man's junk is another man's treasure and takes that very literally. Powered by tales of eBay riches, they are convinced that anything they sell online will make them millions. What this group usually has to offer you is the sort of thing you would typically find at a garage sale or even garbage dump, and 9 times out of 10, it truly is just junk. They offer you old and threadbare clothing with no brand name or other selling point, old pots and pans, a box of empty plastic spray bottles or a coffee tin filled with "vintage" rusted screws. (I have been offered every single one of those items by prospective SA clients, lest you think I'm exaggerating.)

The exciting part of the online auction is that moment of finding surprise value in something originally dismissed as worthless. The unfortunate side effect of this, however, is that it has convinced people like this that it's the rule instead of the rarity and that even true junk has collectible value. Dollar signs in their eyes and tales of so and so's old teapot that sold for $300 on eBay, this group offers you torn clothes, broken home goods, stained mattresses and other things they really ought to be selling at a garage sale, donating, or, in most cases, throwing away. They are under the mistaken impression that anything sold online will be worth far greater than its value.

Pluses

- **Diamond in the rough.** Sometimes there is something of real value in what they offer you, but you'll probably need to dig for it, sometimes literally, in an old barn infested with spiders.

- **Quantity**. This type of client is usually at least some level of packrat. They'll usually have a large number of items and a wide variety of them, so if there's stuff worth selling, there could be lots of it, and it could be older stuff than you'll see from other clients.

Minuses

- **Poor work-to-profit ratio.** The sort of items these clients have often take the most work to clean, research and list and all that work is often not worth what the items sell for.

- **Unrealistic expectations.** These clients are convinced their items are worth much more than they are. In a similar way, these clients are also often very defensive about their items, taking great offense if you refuse them or otherwise indicate that their items aren't worth much.

We'll address this issue in greater detail in the next section, but here's where your knowledge of what sells and what doesn't can be your best friend. Don't invest time or work into any items that aren't worth your time to sell. Only take this sort of client on if you're certain the work is worth the rewards.

MISREPRESENTED ITEMS

At some point over the course of offering your service, you're going to enter into a contract with a client only to discover that you've been misled. Sometimes this is deliberate and the client purposely baited you into the agreement with the promise of one kind of item and then switched it out for something you probably would never have contracted to sell if you'd known the truth. Most of the time, however, this happens innocently out of ignorance or confusion.

A few minutes of misguided internet research has convinced the client that they had this super-rare exclusive collectible, but it's really just the so-common-it's-all-but-worthless version. Or they promise you designer luggage, and it turns out to be a knock-off from the local flea market. Even if their deception isn't on such a high level, clients often exaggerate the quantity, condition, or age of their items, and you'll be the one that suffers from their error.

There are a couple of ways to protect yourself in the event of misrepresented items. The first is to simply head the situation off before it gets to a contract by either going to see the items in person yourself or having the clients send you photographs and detailed descriptions of the items ahead of time. Most unintentional misrepresentation comes when the client is going off their foggy memory of items that may be stored away somewhere and they haven't actually seen them in years. Simply forcing the client to open the boxes and look at the times to photograph or describe them is usually enough for them to revise their description of what they have into something more realistic.

The descriptions you get from your client also help you out in two other ways. It usually gives you enough details about the item to give you a better idea if it's really what they say it is and also serves as a record of what the client promised. Here's where it's a very good idea to insist on a list of each individual item instead of just accepting a general answer. If they promised a "box full of Beatles records" and what you have in front of you is a box with a single Beatles record and 24 random worthless albums, you can take them to task for it. If you've been given items other than what you were promised, you're under no obligation to sell them, especially if they're items that you literally cannot sell online, such as designer fakes or other prohibited items.

If you do find yourself in a situation where you've got items that were misrepresented, and you're stuck selling them, you'll just have to make the best of it. Items of low value that wouldn't sell by themselves often sell when bundled together into a single lot. An item that's banned on your usual marketplace may still be OK to sell on another, and if you end up losing money, think of it as a good reminder to be more careful next time.

EXPECTATIONS, CHALLENGES AND TIPS FOR A SUCCESSFUL CLIENT CONTRACT

While there will always be unforeseen complications, there are a few things you can do from the start to give yourself your best chance at a smooth experience.

- **Manage expectations.** This goes beyond general advice like "under promise and over deliver." Do your best to give your clients a reasonable idea of what to expect from every aspect of the service from how long each step will take, how much money they can expect to make, what your fees will be, and beyond. There is no more frequent culprit behind the unhappy client than the most basic: they expected something other than what you delivered. Make sure you're both on the same page, and you'll both walk away happy.

- **Trust your instincts.** That client has some really great items and you'd make a lot on their commission, but there's just something about them that is making your gut scream, "Run!" While the lure of money is strong, some work is truly not worth the trouble, and if your intuition is throwing up flags, pay attention to it and act accordingly.

- **Keep the lines of communication open.** Be friendly and professional first and foremost, and whenever possible, be honest. Answer emails and reply to phone calls promptly, even if it's just to say that you don't have time to address their concerns at the moment but will in a future message. Keep your clients up to date with every step in their contract. The more often you contact your clients, even if it's with brief messages and updates on little things, the more you increase their trust in you and your service and make them more likely to give you the benefit of the doubt if things go wrong.

- **Do the right thing.** If you're in the wrong, make it right. No one likes admitting when they're wrong, but taking an extra step to both own up to and fix your mistake can regain your client's loyalty and reverberate into great word of mouth and future business.

- **Respect your clients' time.** Your time is valuable, and so it your clients'. Not only should you never waste your clients' time, you should always be respectful of it by apologizing for unexpected delays and doing your best to complete their contract in a timely fashion. While there's a lot that's out of your hands, the parts that are within your control should be completed as promptly as possible. If it's going to take you longer than usual to complete some part of your client's contract, let them know upfront so they can decide if they want to wait it out.

- **Protect yourself.** Have a lawyer go over your contract and get all the terms in writing, even if your client is your mom. It's easy to let things get informal, particularly with a long-term client, but make sure you don't slack on keeping a paper trail just in case.

- **Give both parties an escape clause.** If things start going poorly and you can't seem to right them again, neither you nor the client wants to be stuck with each other until the contract is through. Sometimes it's better to just end things there and cut your losses rather than let the situation get worse. Make sure that walking away is always an option, within reason.

DEALING WITH NIGHTMARE CLIENTS

Despite your best efforts, things will go wrong. I have dozens of horror stories, and you'll probably have your own once you start running your service. While the majority of clients you'll deal with are a genuine pleasure to work with, there are bad bananas in every bunch. The secret is knowing how to deal with them when they do.

First and foremost, no matter how badly your client behaves, you must always stay professional. Not only will this keep you protected if the problem escalates, refraining from personal attacks, no matter how tempting, can often diffuse the situation faster. We unconsciously match our conversation partner, and if you stay calm and cool, your level head will start to rub off on them.

You may get screamed at or chewed out over email. It's a simple thing, but I've often found when dealing with crazy customer of any kind that it works best to just ignore any and all personal attacks and just address the issue behind them. Giving yourself some time between reading or listening to their angry message and composing your reply can also help. An email that seems grossly offensive at first read may just seem a little gruff once you've cooled off. If there's two ways to interpret a message, give the client the benefit of the doubt that they mean it the more positive way and try not to read too much into things. Even if you're wrong and they meant it the worse way, it will help you to craft a better, more measured reply. Never underestimate the power of a genuine apology and good old honesty to remind everyone involved that we're all only human.

As wild as it may seem, a client that is cursing you off and wishing you death one minute, can transform into all sweetness once they've gotten what they want. I've even had nightmare clients turn not only into good repeat customers but also give me some of my best word of mouth all because they liked how I turned the bad situation around. No matter how frustrating it feels at the time, it's worth it to stay on the high road and keep the fallout at a minimum. Because of the local nature of your business, you never want to burn a bridge.

RESEARCH REALISM AND WHEN TO SAY "NO"

One of the most important things that will determine the success of your SA service is knowing what clients to take on and what items to walk away from. Failure to develop this skill results in a poor work-to-profit ratio, and you'll discover yourself working far too hard for the little money you're making. I've spoken to so many sellers who stopped offering Selling Assistance services for this very reason, and they are so ready to blame the concept of selling others' items on commission as the problem without realizing the true cause. You're in control of your service, and that means you're in control of the items you agree to sell. If you take on worthless items, you're going to end up doing a lot of work for little profit, but if you're careful about the items you take on, you'll be able to ensure you're making a fair wage for your work.

Before you take on any client, make sure you've put yourself in a position where you'll make money proportional to the work they'll require. If you're selling items on commission, make sure your research indicates that the items will sell for enough to be worth the time and work needed to list them. If you're working for a flat fee or hourly rate, you've hopefully already built your fee so that you'll make what you need to no matter what the items are, but you'll still want to make sure you're not taking on items that will take more time or work than you've budgeted for.

It's your business. You hold the power. You have the final say in what you will and will not sell, and that alone can determine the success of your business.

RESEARCHING POTENTIAL ITEMS

You'll always want to do at least some research on any items before you list them, no matter how straightforward it seems. One of the simplest ways is to take a look at completed items on the marketplace you plan to list the item on and then supplement this with some web research specific to the item itself. When I call a potential client for a first inquiry, if their item isn't one I'm already experienced with, I like to research their items as they talk, and smartphones make this easier than ever. This way, as the client mentions items to you, you can quickly have an idea of their value and how much work would be involved in listing them in real time. For this same reason, I require new clients to email me a list of what they have so I can make an educated decision about their items before we even decide to meet.

There are hundreds of sites and tools out there that will help you research the potential value of an item. Keep in mind, however, that values can fluctuate based on season, pop culture and demand, so only use your research as a starting point. Sometimes your client's item may look similar to that $20 one at first glance, but a closer look reveals it to be an incredibly rare variety worth hundreds—or the reverse.

Once you've gotten the pricing pulse, how you supplement this info depends on the item. For collectibles, what is this sort of item selling for on the fan message boards and what do the price guides and collector sites say about it? For new items, what's the price point at the big stores like Amazon, Walmart, etc.? If this is a used item, what does it normally sell for new? Do a little digging so you can make an informed guess at how much an item will sell for before you even think about contracting to listing it.

If you're groaning because this sounds like too much work, I have good news. Yes, the first time you sell any given item will be a lot of legwork and research. From that point on, however, you'll start to become so well versed in a variety of items that you'll need to do less and less research. You'll encounter some items so frequently that you likely won't need to research them at all and will know at first glance how they'll sell from experience.

When it comes to research, here are a few other tips:

- **Focus on successful listings.** When researching items on a site like eBay or Etsy, be sure that you're only looking at listings that were actually successfully purchased. The price on an active listing or one that ended without a buyer is no indication of item value. When looking at fan sites or the prices in antique stores, keep in mind that those prices are often wishful thinking and adjust accordingly based on successful sales.

- **Never trust a single sale.** Make sure your price estimates are based on several successful listings as well as a few sources outside your marketplace of choice. If there are 10 completed listings for an item similar to yours and 9 sold for $5 or less but one sold for $50, chances are the $50 one is a fluke, not the norm. But do take the time to look into outliers. If the $50 item has a special characteristic that the $5 ones did not, it's worth knowing to see if the same applies to your item.

- **Manage client expectations.** When giving your client an idea of the value of their item, aim on the lower end of the spectrum and try to avoid giving exact numbers. If you tell a client that an item should sell for between $20 to $40, many will hold you to the $40 you "promised" them. It's better to surprise your client with an unexpectedly higher price than to have them disappointed because no matter how good your research is, the market sometimes has a mind of its own, and especially with auctions, the price is often out of your control.

- **Cover every angle.** When researching an item, try as many different keywords and synonyms as you can think of, seeing which are the most popular based on the number of listings and which most closely match what the client has. For instance, your client may refer to what she has as a footstool, but such an item may more commonly be called an ottoman. You're looking to gather as much info as possible, so you'll need to widen your net to narrow down the details for your item specifically.

What about a client that's got something so rare you can't find a pricing precedent for it? If you're confident that it's worth something, it may be worth the gamble to take it on, especially if it wouldn't be much work to list. You may end up without much for your efforts, but you may get a pleasant surprise.

ITEM REJECTION

When you first begin taking clients as a Selling Assistant, you're mostly looking for practice, and it's tempting to take on every client that contacts you. However, as you build your business and start to have a steady stream of clients, you will need to become more discriminating about what sort of items you take on. Particularly if you're working either on commission or on a fee system based on completed sales, you need to find the right ratio between the time spent on the items versus how much income they earn for you.

The more clients you have, the more your time is worth, and you need to be able to identify which client's items will maximize your profits while minimizing the work involved. You will also want to avoid items that you know will not sell at all, as these are both a waste of your time and a waste of the client's money, as in most cases, you'll still have to pay the listing fees on them. As you familiarize yourself with the SA process, you will eventually be able to evaluate what items are worth your time on the spot, but in the beginning, it will take some legwork.

Here's where your research and experience with past items come into play. It's tempting to agree to sell every item that comes your way, but the key to being a successful SA is being savvy about the items you choose and knowing when to say no. When you're working on commission especially, the amount of money you make is limited by the value of the items you sell. Why waste valuable time prepping and listing items that won't sell for enough to be worth the work?

During your initial interview with the owner, get as many specifics as possible. You need to train your ears to hear the keywords in what they are describing. Find out specifics like brands, condition, their history with the item, dates, etc. I require our new clients to email over a list of the items they have for us to sell with as many details as they can remember to get the conversation started. This list doubles as their item list as part of their contract, so it's something that needs to be done anyway.

Let's take a common example. The client says they have used clothing for you to sell. By itself, that isn't helpful, but if you know that the clothing has either a specific decade style popular for costumes, a desirable vintage look, a major designer brand, or features a logo or brand that is collectible on its own, it could sell well. But if, after talking with the client, you find that what they have is simply no brand clothes from a big box store that didn't even cost much to begin with, you'll know that it will likely not sell and will be a waste of your time.

HOW CAN YOU TELL WHAT SORT OF ITEMS WILL SELL?

Here are some general things to keep in mind, though there are exceptions to every rule:

- **Broken is bad.** As a general rule, most broken items are not worth your time. The exception to this is very large or old items such appliances from the 60s and back that are collectible to restorers or small damage on high-ticket items like original Tiffany lamps. The more the item is worth in perfect condition, the more of that value it retains even when damaged. Whether you sell the item damaged or have it fixed first depends on the items, so do your homework. Buyers of some items would prefer that you have it repaired before you list it for sale, but many collectors would much rather you sell it broken and let them do any restoration themselves than risk you doing it wrong.

- **Even used items hold some value.** Used items that

don't have a major brand name or other draw are unlikely to sell, particularly if they are obsolete and aren't collectible. An item that was expensive new and is still useable, however, will still retain value. For example, you'd have a hard time selling a used VHS since that technology is all but obsolete, but a used treadmill might still be worth selling, since it is both still functional and was also such an expensive item to begin with.

- **Some items will sell in quantity if not individually.** One outfit of no-brand baby clothes might not sell, but a large lot of baby clothes in the same size, even used, might.

- **Keywords are king.** A used bath sponge probably wouldn't sell, but a used sponge featuring Star Wars characters from the 70s is a different story. Items that normally wouldn't sell are more likely to sell if they have a keyword connection that makes them collectible for other reasons.

- **Be wary of media.** Books, records, DVDs and other similar items can be very tricky. With the exception of a few big-name vintage records that are in demand as much for their artwork as their music and collectible first and rare editions of books, most media items are a ton of work to list for very little payoff. Records in particular are difficult to ship and will require the purchase of additional packing supplies. When dealing with a big lot, separate the good stuff out in individual listings and then just sell the rest in a lot to save yourself time.

If you decide to turn away items, be careful how you do it. People take the value of their stuff, even stuff they were planning on getting rid of, very personally. You don't want to burn bridges with a potential client just because you don't want these particular items. I like to blame the market, not their items so it feels less personal. Make it clear to them that while this batch of items aren't a good fit for your selling services for this or that reason, to please let you know what else they find. Give them a better idea of what sort of items you do sell, so they know what to present to you next time and you increase your chances of their hiring you in the future.

What do you do if a client has some great items you'd love to sell but some other real duds? Don't be afraid to reject some items but accept others. If the client has an all or nothing philosophy, weigh the pros of the good items and whether they cancel out the bad. I've been known to take some items I knew weren't worth the work because it enabled me to get at the client's high-value items. But if even the profit off that Coach luggage can't offset those hours of listing Beanie Babies that'll end up selling for pennies, sometimes you just have to walk away.

A good idea is to keep a list of places that accept donations or local consignment shops to recommend. Suggesting another channel for their items increases the chances you'll part on good terms, and the client will approach you with future items or refer you to friends and family.

CLIENT REALISM AND RESERVE PRICES

Owner realism is sometimes the biggest hurdle for the SA. Before you list their items, make sure you have discussed the client's expectations and what they want for the item. For example, let's say the owner has a rare doll. From your research and experience, you know the doll will sell for about $400. The owner, however, refuses to sell for less than $1,000.

This is also an item you will want to reject. If the owner wants an unrealistic amount for the item, you will only be disappointing both of you if you try to do the impossible. It's important to discuss this well before you even contract with the client or list the item and to get this in writing to avoid issues after the fact.

An important element of your contract with your client should be a section in which they indicate the absolute minimum price, their reserve price, that they are willing to take for each item as well as which items they will take any amount for. Make sure they understand that you will try to get more for the item than that whatever figure they give you, but that under that number they are saying they would rather keep the item for themselves. If their minimum price is higher than what you'd be able to sell the item for, then you know not to take it in the first place.

For some reason, the reserve price always throws clients off no matter how I explain it. Invariably, they list a random price they think the item is worth and are then disappointed when I return the item to them saying, "I would have taken less!" I always encourage clients not to list a reserve price unless they are positive they don't want to part with it for a certain price, and I rarely take items with a reserve unless I'm 100% certain I can beat that price.

Often, SA clients have no minimum, they just want to get rid of the items for as much as you can get, and that is great from your standpoint. Just be sure to also get this in writing. A client who told you in person that they don't care what they get for an item can quickly turn into someone who's yelling, "Well, I wouldn't have sold it if I knew it was only going to sell for $10!" Protect yourself by covering these issues upfront and getting them down on paper for extra protection.

CLIENTS AND THEIR ITEMS SUMMARY

Without clients or their items to sell, you'd have no business. Let's take another look at these two vital elements of your Selling Assistant service.

- A Selling Assistant's clients will vary widely and may require their own fee structure or terms as needed.

- Clients come in a variety of types. Understanding them is the key to offering them the best service you can and earning their future business.

- Businesses can be the hardest clients to secure but can

mean steady income for months to years of sales for less work than an individual client.

- Creators working out of their home such as crafters, freelance writers and local musicians are also great opportunities for a lasting partnership that will provide the Selling Assistant with continuous inventory to sell for regular profits.

- The majority of an SA's clients will be individuals and families with items from their homes or personal collections to sell for what is usually a onetime contract but can result in several batches of items over a long period.

- Your best clients will often be those that are either unfamiliar with selling, and thus unable to sell their own items, or those that know how to sell but don't have the time to do it themselves.

- Whether intentional or accidental, every Selling Assistant eventually encounters an item that's been misrepresented.

- For contract success, manage your client's expectations, trust your instincts, communicate well and often, be respectful of your client's time, and protect both yourself and your client with contracts and escape clauses.

- When it comes to difficult clients, stay calm, cool and professional, and you just may turn that bad experience into a lifelong fan.

- The key to a successful Selling Assistant service is knowing when to reject a client's items, and that knowledge comes from research and experience.

- Carefully research your client's items, taking into account outliers, past successful listings and additional study.

- If you don't think that you can sell a client's items, secure their desired price or just don't have time to take on another contract, you'll need to reject their items in a professional way.

- You'll start to get a sense of what kind of items will and won't sell with experience, but until then, remember a few general rules about salability to help you decide which items to take on and which ones to reject.

- Be sure to always manage your client's expectations and encourage them to indicate a reserve price if they have one for a certain item.

MARKETING AND PROMOTION

You're really and truly ready for business now. But how do you reach potential customers? Tomorrow's clients won't even know that you exist unless you start to promote your business today.

Where to begin? Marketing is a massive topic, and there are hundreds, if not thousands, of books on that one topic alone. I can't hope to teach you everything there is to know, and I'm not going to try, but I can give you a general overview and a good foundation to get you started on the right path.

Your biggest hurdle is getting the word out about your SA service and what you do so that someone who's in need of what you offer knows who you are and where to find you. But while that should be your primary focus, the next most important thing to focus on is trust. Once a client has heard of your Selling Assistant services, they aren't going to even consider signing with you unless they have confidence in your abilities and the assurance that their items, and any future profits to be earned from them, are safe in your hands.

While you won't be able achieve both goals with every marketing strategy you employ, you'll want to keep both goals in mind and strive to accomplish both at once whenever possible.

LOCALIZE YOUR MARKETING EFFORTS

Because of the nature of your service, you'll want to concentrate the bulk of your advertising to the same radius you'd be willing to serve for pick-ups or drop-offs. If you're not willing to travel more than an hour to meet with a client, why spend money on advertising beyond that area? While many of the methods we're about to discuss can seem very old-fashioned in a world where the internet rules, the majority of your clients will themselves be old-fashioned by nature so it's appropriate.

TAILOR YOUR MARKETING MESSAGE TO THE TYPE OF CLIENT

The approach you take to marketing your services will vary based on the group that you're trying to reach. You wouldn't use the same method to catch a cat as you would a fish. Marketing is the same way. You're going to tailor your message depending on who you're planning to attract.

Always remember to think like your potential client. We sellers tend to think like sellers without realizing that the outside perspective is completely different. The way you might describe your service with your seller's hat on is unlikely to be the best way to win a client.

Think of the least technology-savvy person you know. Imagine that they've got something to sell and you want to encourage them to use your service. Things you may think of as distinguishing your service might be your e-commerce experience, multiple sales channels or SEO-optimized storefront, but all of that not only would mean nothing to someone without computer skills, it may even turn them off because it makes your service sound more complicated than it really is—or even scary.

Instead of bewildering would-be clients with terms and concepts they know nothing about, you'll often do better by just simplifying everything down to the basics. Focus on the basics of what you'll do, i.e. you'll take their unwanted items and turn them into cash, over the actual details of what your service looks like day to day. You'll sell their items for them on consignment, which means they won't owe you anything until the items sell. Their stuff, plus you, equals money. You're not going to omit or misrepresent anything, just downplaying certain elements to make your service seem simpler and more basic without having to go into the technical details. In other words, to snag a tech-challenged client, you'd want to emphasize the "commerce" part of e-commerce over the "e".

Your marketing messages for a group like this would be things like, "Tired of clutter?" "Is their cash in your attic?" or "Need some extra money?" While you should include your contact info on everything you distribute to market your services, a phone number is key for this group. They're also the most likely to respond to more traditional advertising such as posters and flyers.

On the other side, think of someone who prides themselves on being tech savvy and always has to have the latest gadget. Someone like that may be dazzled by your e-commerce brag list even if they privately don't understand what a word of it means. The quaint, bare bones method described above wouldn't be the best fit to win over a client like that. Instead, you'd need slick copy that makes your service sound cutting-edge. Your message could focus on getting rid of old or obsolete tech while getting money to buy new gadgets or emphasizing the technological aspects of what you do. (Example: "Your items will be optimized for a global market on multiple sales channels to maximize your web profits.") Someone like this is also much more likely to email or text you than ever make a phone call.

What you should take away from this is that marketing is not "one size fits all." You'll eventually have several different marketing messages, and you'll target different groups with each one. While it will mean more work, as you'll be crafting several versions of each campaign, it will be worth it in the end, as you'll score more clients when you speak to them directly with a customized message for their needs.

GO OUT AND FIND THEM

We tend to think of marketing as something we put out into the world and then customers find our ad and come to us. Sometimes, that's how it is, but the average person has never even heard of Selling Assistant services at all and would never even think of hiring you since they don't even know what you do. So, especially in the beginning, you're going to be the one coming to them with your message instead of the other way around.

When it comes to courting corporate clients, freelancers, crafters and other high-yield customers especially, you're going to need a more individualized tactic. Showing up at their door and distributing general marketing materials isn't enough. For the small business clients, you'll need to approach them directly with a pitch tailored specifically to them and their business.

What that will look like depends on the business you're trying to convince to hire you. Will you need to do a slide presentation in front of the president of the company or just spend a few minutes chatting with that guy who's always selling his artwork at the church fair? Will you just give a verbal pitch or have some literature done up, such as a glossy pamphlet that outlines everything you have to offer them?

Unless you've already got a specific contact through your existing networks, this can mean going door to door or cold calling/emailing. Both can be intimidating if you're not a people person, but it's well worth the effort. A single client with a continuous stream of inventory like this can keep you busy and earning income full time even without other clients. Even if the business passes on you right then, they'll know enough about you to keep you in mind for the future if they change their mind or need you for some personal items. So go after them as aggressively as you dare without being annoying and don't forget to follow up. No reply doesn't always mean no. It often just means the right person didn't get a chance to review your message yet.

If the very idea of having to do some in-person selling is repellant to you, consider hiring someone to handle that aspect of it. People with strong sales skills are used to working on commission, and you could offer a similar agreement where you pay them more for interactions that result in a contract than ones that don't. Just make sure they're well versed in what you offer and the terms of your service. The last thing you want is someone making promises for your business that you won't actually be able to keep.

But don't think small businesses are only bulls you need to grab by the horns. Whenever you're chatting with someone who mentions that they need some extra cash or that they have items they want to get rid of, it'd be silly not to give them an informal version of your pitch and leave a business card. My gym membership pays for itself in the number of clients I've snagged through small talk! Most of the time, it feels more like you're offering them help than trying to sell them something, so it's an easy referral to make without any of the potential awkwardness of a sales call.

WORD OF MOUTH

Fortunately, or unfortunately if you anger a client, your Selling Assistance service will be fueled primarily by word of mouth. Word of mouth is simply this: clients you've had in the past will tell others about you in what many consider the most perfect form of advertising. A happy client gushes about you to their friends and neighbors, and some of them contact you on their friend's recommendation. Please those clients and they'll spread the word about your service to their networks, in turn yielding yet more clients and more positive buzz. Soon news of what a great service you run gets passed to more people than you ever possibly could hope to reach on your own, and all of this publicity didn't cost you a cent.

Word of mouth is particularly valuable because it's powerful advertising. People weigh the opinions of their friends and network more heavily than the opinions of strangers, so they're that much more likely to look into your service. Of course, if a positive experience can reverberate into that much good business, imagine the damage a negative one can do!

While you may find yourself doing a lot of marketing in the beginning, once you've secured that first wave of clients, you'll find that most of your second wave will be the friends, family, neighbors and co-workers of that first group and so on. Many times, I've reached a point in my service when I didn't need to do any advertising at all, as I had plenty of word-of-mouth business to keep me busy without taking on any new clients. When the flow of work begins to slow, you can simply pick your marketing efforts back up again as needed.

The most important thing to remember about this, however, is the famous cliché: a happy customer tells two people, but an unhappy customer tells ten. You want to make sure to keep your customers happy because negative word of mouth can spread much faster than positive and can seriously cripple your business efforts. A simple way to always end a business relationship on a good note is to send a small gift at the end of your contract with a note stating how you appreciate their business. Make sure to include a few business cards and mention that if they know of anyone else with items to sell, you would appreciate your sending them your way.

When you're first starting out, one of the smartest things you can do is offer your service at a discount to close friends and family. They'll be more understanding both because they know you're still learning and because they're getting such a good deal. This makes it all the easier for you to wow them with your service. If everyone in this practice group tells even a single a friend about your service, you'll have dozens of new clients from that alone with no additional advertising.

Word of mouth is something that happens organically, and you can't really control it. But you can increase the likelihood of people spreading positive reviews by giving your customers the best experience possible and staying professional and personable. If you want to encourage clients to recommend your service to their friends, a referral bonus is a simple incentive to add.

REFERRAL BONUS

Since word of mouth is an SA's most useful marketing tool, you may want to encourage clients to refer others to you by offering a bonus for passing the word on. Though this may sound like an intimidating process, all it really entails is creating a reward for current or former clients when they send you a new client that results in a successful contract. If you find it difficult to get word-of-mouth referrals, you may want to give it a try. If the increase in new clients offsets the cost of giving the bonus, it could be great for business.

The specifics of your referral program are up to you. Cash bonuses are attractive, but you can award any kind of prize or bonus. Just make sure to write out the terms of the referral program very clearly to avoid quibbling. It could be part of your initial client contract or a separate document.

Some possibilities you can consider are:

- Offer a single flat cash bonus upon signing the referred client to a contract.

- Offer the referring client a percentage of or tiered bonuses based on any profits made on the resulting contract.

- If the referring client is still a current client, offer them a reduced fee or commission based on their successful leads.

Word of mouth happens organically regardless of any incentive program you may invent, but a client who otherwise may never have considered referring your services is more likely to tell their friends and networks when they know they're getting something in return. If an official referral program seems too complicated, you can, and should, reward clients that make referrals in other ways. If a client does refer a good client to you, send them a small gift such as flowers, candies, etc. to show your appreciation. Clients will appreciate this and be encouraged to refer more in the future.

WORKSHOPS, CLASSES AND OTHER EVENTS

Even if you aren't offering tutoring or other paid selling lessons as part of your business, workshops and classes are one of the best ways to advertise your service, and they cost nothing other than time. Simply getting to spend some time with you, even if it's in a classroom setting and not one-on-one, can greatly increase trust and make attendees that much more likely to sign up for your service or even recommend you to others without ever having used you themselves. Offering a free class can be a big local draw, especially if there's not much going on at the venue or in your area as a whole.

It's also a great marketing opportunity because people will come to learn what you have to teach and, in turn, learn about your services. The venue will usually advertise your event ahead of time, and you'll also get the benefit of their marketing, which will reach many more people than will actually attend the event itself. Even small venues promote their events with things like posters, on their website, in email list, on their public events calendar or in online and print media. You'll discover that simply having heard of you in connection with a venue they're affiliated with is often sufficient to increase someone's faith in you enough to take the next step and hire you.

No matter how much marketing the venue itself does, however, you'll still want to promote it heavily yourself. Whenever possible, also get local friends and family to come to increase attendance. The better attended your program is, the more likely they will ask you back to do another in the future, and then you can use those numbers to get other venues to invite you in as well.

Many community gathering places, such as libraries, churches or senior centers, are always looking to fill their events calendar, so most will jump at your offer of a free program for their patrons. In exchange for plugging a hole in their schedule, you'll get the space to hold your class. You'll increase your chances of their having you back if there's an incentive for the venue itself such as a bonus for how many clients result from the event. Other areas known for being SA friendly that will sometimes let you hold classes are your local post office, UPS or FedEx retail locations, or business centers like PostNet and MailBoxes etc., especially if you're a customer of theirs and frequent their services.

Whenever possible, get your host location involved and invested in your event. Could you do Antiques Roadshow, Tupperware-style parties where everyone can bring their items for you to evaluate and the host can earn referral bonuses for every new contract? Can you tailor your lesson to feature the resources of the library that gave you the room for your event? Can you sell something at the event, such as a book or other paid service, that the venue could take a cut of?

When it comes to the locations themselves, let your existing network inform where you start your search. If you've got a personal connection to someone in your community with a space that would work for a class, approach them even if the relationship to your service isn't immediately clear. There's an angle for promoting your service to just about any group you can imagine, you just need to find it. Your buddy who sells photography equipment might be willing to let you have a class in her store about taking great pictures for selling online, especially if you tailored it to recommend the types of items she sells, so it's marketing for both of you. Your cousin's motorcycle gang might be interested in a class on how to sell some of their old bike parts. Your uncle's pizza parlor might want to host a Pizza Profits night where anyone who buys a slice gets to attend your class on earning extra cash for free.

If community venues and your network connections fail you, you can always pay to rent a space. While that's an extra expense, it may be worth it if the class yields a good number of new client contracts. Paying for the space does ensure that you have more control over your event without any outside restrictions.

Should host an event in your home? Only as a last resort, and if you can ensure that you'll be able to still present yourself and your business in the most professional way possible. Having an event in a private residence is actually more of an attendance deterrent than it is a danger for you because there isn't the perceived safety of a public space.

BUT WHAT TO TEACH?

The most obvious thing is teaching how to sell online. You can either do a general overview or just specialize the lesson down to a single marketplace, such as just selling on eBay Motors or Etsy depending on your audience. But if you teach people how to sell online themselves, won't they not need your service then? Maybe. But in most cases, they'll realize how much work it is, and that will make them even more likely to hire you in the future.

If you're worried that teaching your audience to fish will put your seafood market out of business, there are still many classes you can teach that subtly recommend your services while still providing value on their own. Here's some examples to get you started:

- **Cash in your attic.** This would be a class that emphasizes looking around your house for items that would be the best fit to sell online. You could go over the types of items that are collectible and sell well today. While ostensibly this lesson is to help your students best choose which of their items they should try selling online, it's also turning them into ideal clients if they decide to hire you because they'll already know what kind of items to present you.

- **The beginner's guide to buying online.** In this type of class, you'd teach the basics of buying online and how people can get the best deals. This would appeal to a wide variety of people, and especially to those technology-challenged types that are the most likely to need your service. Once they understand how the e-commerce process works, even if it's just from the buyer's side, they'll be that much more likely to consider hiring you to sell their items for them that way.

- **Internet safety and security when buying online.** Similar to the one above, this time you'd focus on the things people most fear about e-commerce and address some of their more basic concerns like passwords, secure payment processing and buyer and seller protection. And you could end by pointing out that if they are still concerned about their privacy, they could always hire someone to do their selling for them, and guess who offers that service?

- **Shipping secrets for cheaper mailing.** You've picked up a wide variety of tips on how to mail things cheaply and effectively as a seller, so it would be easy to share some of them. Anyone looking to save some money shipping could also use a little extra cash from selling their items, which dovetails nicely into your service.

You may not realize you're already an expert on a variety of topics tangentially related to selling online that nicely refer your service without being overtly a commercial. Just be careful when doing multiple local classes and try to vary the topic from location to location. Not only will this encourage people to attend more than one session, letting each class advertise the next one, it will also ensure each venue is getting their own unique event and make them more likely to have you back.

As with any marketing, you don't have to do this all the time. Whenever your flow of clients slows, offer some classes and then, once your work volume is back up where you want it, you can stop until needed again.

PRESS RELEASES

Wouldn't it be great to get your service some press coverage? You may think that's out of your price range, but it's actually something you secure for close to free. All you need is a good press release.

A press release can be one of the simplest, cheapest and most effective ways of marketing your SA services. The best press release is basically an ad for your service cleverly disguised as news article. Newspapers, websites, magazines, TV and radio stations love press releases because they can print or read them as a news story without having to write anything themselves while you get what would normally be expensive media coverage for free. However, bloggers, reporters and broadcasters are all bombarded with thousands of press releases each day, so to have a chance, you've got to make your release stand out.

While you can find a wealth of info online about crafting a good press release, here are some basic tips to get you started. You'll be writing the press release in the third person as if someone else is writing it, so instead of "I offer…" it's "Joe Smith offers…" Never use the first person unless it's part of a quote. Incorporate quotes from both yourself and testimonials from your clients into your release whenever possible.

Triple check for typos before sending your release out. Have several people read it over to catch what you miss. A poorly written release is worse than not sending one at all. In fact, if you're not sure if you can write a good enough release on your own, it's well worth the investment to hire someone to do it. Hiring a freelance writer or editor is much less expensive than you might think and can make a huge difference in a lot of elements of your business. You may even be able to barter for what you need, giving your Selling Assistant services for free in exchange for the freelancers expertise.

A quick internet search will reveal hundreds of press-release templates. When it comes to all marketing materials, but especially press releases, I'd advise only using templates for inspiration. The most effective marketing materials will be the ones that you either create or hire someone to create specifically for your business.

A press release will either be printed or read as is, used to write/spark an entirely new article or editorial or lead to an interview with you. Making sure your current contact information (telephone and email) is on the release is a must. The reporter or editor with your press release needs to be able to contact you for an interview or more information if they're interested in your story. Make sure you're monitoring the contact info you posted in the days following your release closely so you don't miss an opportunity. Everyone in news media is always on a deadline, and a prompt reply can mean the difference between a feature and nothing.

Once you've got your release, submit directly to all the local media that serve your area. Check the website or call each radio station, newspaper or other publication for their submission guidelines before sending. The better you follow their directions, the more likely they'll run your story. Making up a contact list will take some time, but you only need to do it once and can use it for every release you do in the future. While you can pay to have your release distributed online, with local media, you're actually better off sending it yourself. Send out individualized messages to each contact too—no mass emails or bulk mailings. Be professional but persistent and follow up if you don't get a reply.

Lastly, a press release is not a one-time thing. Two months is about the time it takes media outlets to forget about a story, so you need to make sure you stay in their memories without being overbearing. Tweak your release to give it a new angle so it stays fresh and send a new version out several times a year. Whenever possible, customize it to take advantage of trending news stories or timely keyword.

Can't seem to get coverage? Many local news sites allow you to have a blog right on their site. Post your release there, and it may later get picked up as a story.

PAPER GOODS

Hanging posters and leaving business cards or flyers in public locations is a great way to bring in new customers, but be sure to get the permission of the location first. Your materials should not only include a brief summary of what your service does but also your contact info, especially a phone number if you have one. Whenever possible, also include a link to your website where potential clients can review the terms and details of your service before they commit to calling you. For best results, also include a call to action or a promotion, such as a coupon code or other special offer. It not only adds extra value to your handout and makes people more likely to pick your materials up, it also increases the likelihood of them actually contacting you.

Areas where people know you personally or are at least familiar with you are your best bets. Consider including your photo on your flyer because the people at your gym, church, supermarket etc. may know your face but not necessarily remember your name. Even if a person has never seen you before in their life, even the slightest local connection can give you an edge over a SA or other consignment service that feels unfamiliar.

While every community is different, here's a few ideas to get you started:

- Senior centers and retirement homes
- Social clubs and community halls
- Libraries
- Churches
- Grocery stores
- Cafés, coffee shops and other eateries

- Gyms and fitness clubs, especially those that cater to older patrons, such as the chain Curves for Women

- Daycare centers

- Office complexes or supply stores

- Commuter stations (bus stops, parking garages, train platforms, etc.)

- Self storage or anywhere people pay to store things you could sell for them

If you find yourself stuck for ideas, try to put yourself in your clients' minds and picture where they go over the course of their day. Also, keep in mind that each location is targeting a different type of client and adjust your marketing accordingly. The person seeing your flyer in the coffee shop may be unemployed and looking for the extra cash your service could get them, while the person at the daycare center may have a greater need for more time with their family or to get rid of some clutter to free up some space.

The biggest downside to physical marketing materials is the cost, but you can manage this if you're savvy. A site like Vista Print will give you customized paper goods like business cards and postcards for the just the cost of shipping, as long as they can put their ad on the back. Also, keep an eye on coupon sites like Retail Me Not for deals. Office supply stores with print shops and online stationary companies both run special offers and other promotions that can give you the chance to get your marketing materials printed up for a big discount or even free if you order at the right time.

FUNDRAISERS AND TRICKY TRAYS

Another great way to connect with your local community and let them know about your service is through fundraisers and similar local events. Just about every church, school or club holds some kind of fundraising event at least once a year. Many of these events rely on donated items to either auction off or give as prizes. A simple way to get the word out about your services is to have your business donate to as many of these local events as you can find.

What you donate is up to you. It could be a gift certificate entitling the winner to $50 off your usual fee or commission. It could be a voucher for a free sample class if you offer tutoring. Your donation could entitle them to having their first 5 items listed for free, where you'd waive all fees and commission.

Donating to fundraisers is as close to a win-win situation as you can get in marketing. The only cost of this is the effort it takes you to deliver on what you donated, and that's assuming the winner ever redeems the prize, which they often never do. The group will usually list your company name and url in the event program as a sponsor and will sometimes even leave your flyers or other marketing materials out on guest tables or stuff them in guest goodie bags, widening your reach. In addition, anyone deciding what to bid on or which giveaway to enter will read about your services when considering your prize, so even if they don't win, they are likely to look you up to possibly hire you later anyway.

Though you will be doing the labor for the winner for free or giving them a discount on that first item or items, they will often give you more items to sell than their prize covered, so you'll still earn income on their contract. As long as they're pleased with your services, you may get them or anyone they refer as a full paying customer once their certificate is used up.

More importantly, because you're contributing to a local cause, this gives you positive buzz in your community, which can translate into more contracts and word of mouth for your business regardless of the outcome of your donation itself.

PRINT ADS, COUPON BOOKS AND MAILERS

As your business expands, particularly if you've opened a physical storefront, you may want to consider placing ads in the local newspapers or coupon mailer. Placing a coupon in your ad is a great way to not only track your marketing efforts, but also to give potential clients an extra incentive to try out your services. As with a donation prize, this can be as simple as a discount or waived commission. Newspaper ads and coupon mailers can be very expensive, however, so you may want to consider less expensive alternatives such as the church bulletin, free local paper, high school newsletter, community theatre program or placemat at the local diner. Ads like these are almost always fundraisers for the organization or small business, so their supporters are all the more likely to patronize your business as a thanks for supporting theirs. If you're doing both coupon advertising and donating to fundraisers, however, always be sure that whatever you offer as a prize to the fundraisers is a substantially better offer than the deal on your coupons or you'll end up burning bridges with the fundraising organizations and their patrons. If what you're donating is no better than the coupon everyone else gets, it devalues it substantially.

Should you go all out and spring for television advertising, billboards or radio ads? As your business grows, you may want to give this a shot, but when you're starting out, it's a mistake. Most of the ideas we've already gone over are either very low cost or free, while things like billboards are incredibly expensive with a lower conversion rate, and it's much harder to make that money back. Give some of these free or lower cost options a try first.

ONLINE MARKETING

If you're working on building a global or even national SA business where clients can mail you their items from anywhere, advertising online is essential. But even if you're keeping your SA business local, it's a mistake to ignore the internet. With the domination of smartphones and tablets, even your neighbor is more likely to find your business through Google than your garden party.

YOUR WEBSITE

You should really have a website for your SA service, even if it's a very basic one using free hosting such as Google Sites or a free blog from Blogger or Wordpress.com. At the least, you need a place to direct buyers to find a description of your service, your contact info and to answer some of your most frequently asked questions. This could also showcase some of your features such as drop-off hours or a schedule of classes and workshops you offer. A photograph of yourself and some testimonials from past clients can increase client trust even before you speak a word with them.

Most importantly, when you have a website, you have a single destination to direct potential clients or media that answers all their questions about your service. Not only does this make you look more professional, it should save you time since you'll have to answer fewer questions when you sign a client who visited your site first. Lastly, a website gives browsers a passive way to find out about your service before they commit to a conversation, and for many introverted types, this can be a huge selling point.

SOCIAL NETWORKING

While social networking can be a time suck, it takes minutes to set up a simple page on sites like Twitter, Facebook and Google+ for your business with the basics about your service. Social pages often rank higher in search engines than anywhere else, so it may well get you eyeballs you wouldn't otherwise get. No matter how you personally feel about social media, there's no denying that a majority of the population uses sites like Facebook, and not having a presence for your business on there is a mistake.

Once you get your basic info up, you should really share something on your page at least once a week so that it always looks active if a prospective client peeks in. If you've got a blog, it's a simple matter to have those posts automatically share on your business pages, and services like Buffer let you write up as many posts as you want ahead of time and queue them up so the page stays active even if you haven't looked at it in days. Of course, ideally, you'll use those pages to engage your customers and build up your brand, but realistically, simply having an active presence of any kind is often enough for a local service such as yours to generate leads.

LOCAL LISTINGS

Almost every major search engine has a section geared towards local businesses so get yourself listed in as many of them as you can, especially the big ones like Facebook, Yahoo, and Google. There are also sites like Yelp that offer local listings and reviews, and there may be other options that are specific to your region. It's important to get into these listings not only because it will let prospective clients find you more easily but also because it lets past customers and clients leave you, hopefully positive, reviews, which can boost your business more than the best marketing ever could.

ONLINE KEYWORD ADS

These services, such as Google Adwords or Facebook Ads, involve setting up a budget per month that bids on certain keywords. When displaying the search results for these keywords, your ad will show. You can opt to pay either by the impression or by the clicks. Your best bet is to keep your keywords targeted locally so you're not wasting your money on clicks outside your region, and most advertising platforms will let you specify an area when you set up your campaign. If you've got a local listing within the same search engine you're advertising on, you'll get even more value for your dollars and preferential placement over an external website.

Pay Per Click (PPC) ads such as this tend to be hit or miss. For some people they are a godsend; for others, they are a waste of money. Your mileage may vary, but it's inexpensive to experiment. Set a small budget before you commit a lot of funds to a campaign and make sure you have a way to track your conversions to see if it's worth the cost. If your web host or other provider gave you free advertising credits to use, as many do, all the better since you can test drive for free.

With a little experimentation, you may find it to be a very cost-effective way to get new clients. If not, tweak your settings until it is or walk away. There's lots of other ways to get the word out.

TAKE ADVANTAGE OF YOUR EXISTING NETWORK

Make sure you've put a small description of your service and link to your website wherever you already have a presence online, even if it's a personal presence. While sites like eBay won't let you link directly to an external webpage in your listings, take full advantage of pages where they do such as the About Me and My World pages. Do you have a blog? A personal LinkedIn, Twitter, Facebook, or other networking profile? A personal website? An instant messaging profile? Make sure you mention your SA service everywhere you are.

Many of my clients have been friends and acquaintances who would rather hire me to sell their items or send their friends and family my way because we have a personal connection over someone who might be more local to them or even a better fit for their items. Your social network and existing relationships are your most valuable assets, and if they don't realize what you offer, you're just cheating yourself out of those opportunities. That's not to say you should spam your friends, but having a discrete mention of your service or occasionally offering a "friends and family only" deal is a great way to make the people you already know in real life one of your best marketing tools.

MARKETING TIMING

All too often, you're feeling full of fire and inspired to do some marketing so you just quickly do it right then without thinking about your promotion as part of the big picture. Why waste your advertising dollars just because you were a little too eager? Taking the time to consider every step before you do it will save you money in the long run.

Firstly, consider the volume of business you're currently experiencing. You don't want to start a huge marketing campaign at a time when you're already swamped with work. What a shame it would be to turn new clients away because you don't have the time for them now.

Secondly, keep the calendar in mind. A promotion you run to coincide with the coming of spring could be hugely successful because it coincides with the annual ritual of cleaning when people are usually looking to get rid of some stuff. That same promotion could fail miserably, however, if you ran it during the end of the year when people are too busy with the melee of the winter holidays to be thinking about what's in their attic. There's always going to be certain points in the year that lend themselves more than others to your SA service.

In general, it comes down to thinking every advertising move out thoroughly before taking the plunge. Not only will this keep you from wasting money, it will also give you the best result from the money you do spend. Taking the time to highlight the best times for your marketing a few months in advance doesn't take long and can save you from missing opportunities.

MARKETING MAIN POINTS

Promoting your service can seem daunting, but once you've got a few ideas to get you started, you'll start to see opportunities everywhere. Be careful with your advertising dollars and take advantage of free opportunities whenever possible. Every new person who hears about your business is another potential client and source of word of mouth.

Let's review some of the ideas we covered in this section.

- It's not enough to get the word out about your services,

you'll also need to educate potential clients who've never even heard of Selling Assistance on what your service is and does.

- You'll gain their business by gaining their trust, but pricing is a factor too.

- Localize your marketing efforts to the area you plan to serve so you're not wasting money advertising to clients out of your area.

- There is no one size fits all! Tailor your marketing to attract different demographics by tailoring your marketing messages to each group.

- While your marketing will draw smaller clients to you, when it comes to big-fish clients like businesses, freelancers and creators, you may need to go to them.

- Organic, word-of-mouth advertising will be the best way to quickly spread word of your business, so make sure you're getting the best reviews possible by always offering exemplary service.

- Encourage prior customers to tell a friend about your service by offering a bonus for sending you a new client.

- Offer free workshops, classes and other events in your area to attract locals to both get to know you and consider your service.

- Regularly send out press releases, tweaked to keep them timely and relevant, to score media coverage like radio, newspapers, news websites and television.

- Distribute paper goods like postcards, business cards and flyers wherever your target customers are likely to congregate.

- Donate to local fundraisers and tricky trays to attract members of those organizations and their supporters to check out your service.

- Consider taking out an ad or placing a coupon in local

staples such as the placemat at the diner, high school coupon book or the community play program over a higher profile, but more expensive, publication like a commercial coupon magazine.

- Set up a website for your service, even if it's on a free site, to have a professional space where potential clients can consider your service and answer their questions before even connecting with you.

- Maintain an active social media presence to connect with potential clients and help them to discover your service.

- Get your business listed in Yellow Page type services online that serve your region to make sure locals can find you.

- Consider Pay Per Click ads as an inexpensive way to target local customers and make them aware of the services you offer.

- Take advantage of your existing networks by making sure your friends and family are aware of what your service does by offering occasional deals or mentions, not spamming or being annoying.

- Plan your marketing out and pay attention to timing so you're never wasting your time and efforts doing a big campaign at the wrong time.

WHAT IS RUNNING A SELLING ASSISTANT BUSINESS ACTUALLY LIKE?

Before we go into the technicalities of running a business like this, let's take a moment, human to human, to go over the real-life realities of becoming a Selling Assistant. I have spent two decades selling other people's items for them, and while your experiences can and will vary, I feel like I can give you at least a glimpse into what you can expect. Here's my warts-and-all review of what working as a SA is really like.

Let's start with what I really love about it.

MAKING MONEY FOR YOURSELF WHILE MAKING MONEY FOR OTHERS

My SA business didn't start out as a business but rather as a network of favors. Friends and family would ask if I would please sell an item for them and insist on my taking a cut of the sale price as a thanks for my work. Even as I started to build up my service and take on clients from outside my social circles, I found that there was something very satisfying about making money by helping others to make money.

How does a normal small business make their first profits? It usually involves hitting up the people they already know to be their first customers. A landscaper goes door to door or puts up a sign asking neighbors to hire her to do their yard. Writers beg their friends and family to buy their books. The restaurateur nags his Facebook friends to come eat at his pizzeria.

We've all been on the receiving end of this, and it's uncomfortable for both parties. It's awkward enough marketing a new business without the added element of putting a financial burden on your existing social relationships and local community. Not only will it tax those relationships, it can make you resent your friends who don't support your business even though, rationally, you know they owe no obligation.

Even when your customers are strangers, there's still an element of this. Without people to hire you, you don't make any income. Your success still depends on other people giving you their hard-earned money.

A Selling Assistant doesn't experience any of this.

With a Selling Assistant service, your clients rarely give you any money up front, so you aren't imposing on them to help your business get started. They give you items, and your payment comes from the subsequent sale of those items. Even when you subtract your fees or commission from the final sale price, your client still almost never has to pay you anything out of their pocket. In turn, you're giving them extra cash in exchange for the items they no longer wanted. Asking your friends if they're looking to get rid of any junk or could use some extra cash is much easier than asking for their money!

Whenever our economy is in a slump, my Selling Assistant business is still booming. The reason is simple: I offer people a way to earn some extra cash in exchange for things they didn't want anyway, which is something everyone can use no matter what the economic climate is like. I don't have to beg people to give me their hard-earned income, they approach me because they're either looking for money or to get rid of a few items themselves, and they know my service can get it for them.

This is, by far, one of the best things about being a Selling Assistant. I can finish a very profitable contract with a client where I made thousands of dollars and the client ends up thanking me like I did them a huge favor. And, in a way, I did. Maybe I not only helped her clear out all her unwanted items, I also made her enough money so she can go on that cruise she and her husband wanted for their anniversary. There's something very satisfying about providing a service that is mutually beneficial to both you and your client. As a Selling Assistant, the success of your business depends on how much money you earn for other people, so it lets you make money for yourself while making money for others.

AUTONOMY, FREEDOM AND FLEXIBILITY OF TIME AND TERMS

The Selling Assistant is her own boss, sets her own hours, draws up her own terms and controls her own workflow. Selling Assistants answer to no one, agree to no terms, and are bound by no contracts they don't create themselves. You have the freedom to set up your service entirely on your own terms. For me this has meant that I can turn down SA jobs I don't want to take, take a break from SA services whenever I want to without having to request permission from anyone, or adjust my service policies on the fly if I notice something isn't working.

The other advantage is the incredible flexibility this offers. Few business opportunities provide this much autonomy, and this makes it easy to adapt a SA business to full or part time as needed. When I was in high school, I did SA work as a part-time job after school and on weekends while my peers worked at fast food and retail places. When I later moved to college, my SA business became seasonal, and I only offered the service over school breaks when I was home. Other than client meetings, which should probably happen during normal hours, the time of day you do the job is entirely up to you, so it's possible to do this service late at night while the kids are in bed, around your day job or whenever fits your schedule.

This adaptability opens starting a SA business to anyone with regular computer access regardless of their walk of life. Retirees looking for a little extra money, stay-at-home parents who want something that fits around a busy activity schedule, students who want a flexible part-time job, teachers looking for seasonal work, the unemployed looking for work that won't interfere with job interviews... a Selling Assistant business can serve all those groups and more. I can't think of a single other business opportunity, let alone one you can do from your home, with that much freedom.

REQUIRES LITTLE TO NO MONEY TO START UP

While there are things you can and should do before you start offering your service, such as registering your business, even they are recommended and not strictly necessary expenses. You could start taking on client items right now without having to spend a dime. OK, sure, you may pay listing fees on those first few items depending on your marketplace, but as long as your items sell before your invoice comes due, that will be money out of profit, not pocket.

Contrast this with most other small business opportunities where you'll need lots of start-up cash. In many cases, you'll even need to take out a loan to get started. The fact that you could take on a client today without spending much, or anything at all, is very attractive. After all, if you had gobs of money just lying around, you wouldn't be looking for a way to earn more if it!

FANTASTIC RESUME BUILDER

Starting your own Selling Assistant business looks better on your work history than just about any part-time job you could take, and it certainly looks better than an unexplained resume gap such as unemployment. Students take note, degree be damned, I've spent more time in job interviews answering questions about my Selling Assistant business than anything else on my rather accomplished resume, and it's landed me many posts over the years, even in fields completely unrelated to e-commerce. Running a successful customer-oriented business, even part time, shows you have gumption, management, organization and people skills that stand out in any interview situation.

THE REALITIES OF SELLING ONLINE

The advantages of selling over the internet are many, and over the years, sites like eBay have fine-tuned many parts of the process to make it faster and easier for sellers. The eBay I started selling on the 90s looks like a clunky cousin to the efficient process a seller experiences today. There are literally hundreds of tools that make the listing and selling process faster and more efficient. Bulk listing tools, third-party services and a wealth of information available online can make even the most wide-eyed newbie a seasoned professional in a short amount of time.

Most marketplaces also have so many regular browsers and visitors that your items will usually find their buyers even if you do no outside promotion. This is the main reason eBay remains the king of collectibles and Etsy the lord of handmade no matter how many clones or rivals websites pop up. Other sites may have lower fees or other gimmicks, but they have the eyeballs of buyers and that usually translates into faster sales for a higher price. Another thing that should not be discounted is the affiliate programs on sites like eBay, Half.com and Amazon, which ensures that bloggers and other content providers around the web are helping to promote the items you sell.

But if you've already sold items online, then you know some the challenges of each marketplace. Even without taking on the items of others, selling itself comes with its own set of considerations, so be sure you understand the realities of each platform and marketplace before diving in. I've been selling on eBay since 1997, and while I know it's a powerful tool that has helped me to build my business and earn a income working from home, I'll also be the first to admit that I spend a lot of time very annoyed with them for the idiotic things they do. (There's a reason my blog is called TheWhineSeller.com.) I don't think there's a single seller out there that's 100% satisfied with their current selling solution.

Any marketplace or platform will have policies you'll have to adhere to, and those will change from time to time. Meeting them can be a challenge, especially when these changes force you to alter the terms of your Selling Assistant service or limit how you do business. Every e-commerce option also charges some kind of fees, and those can eat into your profits. Selling online can be time-consuming and a lot of work, especially when you're first starting out and haven't developed an efficient routine. Luckily, there is a host of third-party listing services and tools to take some of the time burden off your shoulders, though many come with additional costs.

Beyond your platform itself, selling online includes dozens of other external factors that can be both pluses and minuses on their own. For instance, customers can be a joy or a nightmare, and that will vary from sale to sale. Shipping items means dealing with shipping providers and the challenges of packaging and transport. You may love the ease and speed of your payment processor one day but be out for blood the next when they have that outage in the middle of your biggest sales night.

The challenges of starting and running your own Selling Assistant business come part and parcel with understanding the process of e-commerce. I have found that eBay's little foibles are well worth the effort for the end result, and you too many find that special marketplace where, once you've mastered the nuances of the site, you appreciate it as a powerful platform and money-making tool even while you love to hate it.

REALITIES OF A HOME-BASED BUSINESS

Admit it. It's the work-from-home aspect of working as a Selling Assistant that got you to pick up this book in the first place, isn't it? I've seen the pop-up ads, the email spam, and the make money in your pajamas scams, and I know that working out of your house is a dream for a lot of people. When I first decided to leave my regular 9-to-5 office job to concentrate on my business full time, I was right there with you, thinking about how much I'd save on work clothes, in gas and travel, and in buying lunch by working at home.

We tend to think about working from home as the magic solution to everything we hate about working in an office without realizing that working from home comes with its own unique set of problems. While working from home can be an excellent way to earn an income, and it does give you more flexibility, it's important to look at the realities of running a home-based business. Of course, a Selling Assistant service can be run from anywhere, and your SA service may eventually grow to be a brick and mortar drop-off consignment store, but the majority of Selling Assistants at least start by working out of their homes, so it's important to consider what you're getting into.

At eBay Live in 2007, one speaker asked a large room full of sellers, "How many of you started your own business because you wanted more freedom?" Nearly everyone in the room held up their hand. He continued, "And you got freedom, didn't you? The freedom to work any 80 hours a week you want!"

I re-told this story to a woman at my gym, and her dreamy response was, "It must be so nice to have that freedom." She missed the point of the joke, missed the fact that 80 hours a week is a ridiculous amount of time to work and heard only what she wanted to hear: that working from home was wonderful and gave you freedom. I mention this because I have a horrible feeling you're like this woman, and I want to shake the stars out of your eyes and make sure that you're looking at this clearly.

When you first think about running your own home-based business, many people picture themselves glancing at a laptop once a day while passing the hours away sprawled in leisure, a fruity drink in their hand. Oddly enough, when people start to think about working from home, they focus on all the pluses of "at home" and forget completely about the "work" element. Yes, there is freedom to working from home, but it comes at a price and requires self-discipline to make work.

There are certainly advantages to a home-based business. Forget the planes, trains and automobiles, getting to work is much simpler when you're already there! Not having to commute also means that each time the gas prices go up, it feels like you just got a raise. You can indeed work in your pajamas as long as you aren't meeting clients. You're home for those that need you to be, be they pets, aging parents or young children.

But working from home is just as much work, if not more, as working at a normal job. There are many more distractions, including family, housework, television, and pets. Being your own boss also means that you need to be able to self-motivate, have good organizational and time-management skills and be able to work no matter what's going on in the background.

Some people can't handle it. They succumb to the pleasures of television, the call of the laundry, or a burning desire to organize their sock drawers, often doing just about anything but work. Having children or a spouse who is home only adds to the distractions and increases the need for you to block everything out and get to work.

I've always struggled with the opposite problem. Without the physical separation you get when you leave your office to come home, I feel like I am always at work. I often find myself working way too much or not stopping after a reasonable amount of time. It's hard to enjoy a relaxing dinner on the same kitchen table you spent all day working at unless you start to teach yourself to separate your work from your home life. This is often easier said than done.

Working from home can also be very lonely. It's easy to underestimate the value of co-workers and the affect socialization has on our general well being. Social networking helps but not seeing another human face to face for hours to days at a time can take its toll.

There is a certain stigma associated with working from home that seems to come directly from that perception of working from home being a relaxing vacation. Family and friends often have difficulty understanding that working from home is real work. Spouses may not understand why you couldn't do this or that since you "just sat home all day." Friends want to know why you can't just take off and have lunch with them whenever you want. Kids and pets also have a lot of trouble understanding why, if you're home, you can't play with them.

But this is typical of how most people view working from home. You will be working hard to build a company, and even those closest to you picture you sitting around doing nothing. You aren't going to be able to change perceptions about a home-based business, and it's not worth trying, but I included this section to make sure that you were not under any illusions before you embarked on this journey.

LOTS OF CUSTOMER AND CLIENT INTERACTION

Do you consider yourself a people person? How do you deal with difficult people? A Selling Assistant deals with clients and needs to manage not only their items but also their expectations of your service. At the same time, as a seller, you'll be regularly dealing with customers, many of whom believe the old adage that they are always right. Any time money is involved, even interactions that seem routine can become a challenge to keep smooth.

Being a SA is very customer-service oriented, and working with both clients and customers can be frustrating at times. Of course, it can also be incredibly rewarding. If you and your client share a passion for the same items, you may find yourself truly enjoying that contract.

Either way, while much of the SA service is done while alone in front of a computer or tablet screen, understand there's plenty of interaction with several very different types of customers that you'll have to manage.

THE CARE AND STORAGE OF CLIENT ITEMS

If you decide, as many SAs do, to keep the items for the owner while they're on sale, storage for the items can quickly become an issue. The first challenge is finding the space for it all. No sooner do you reclaim the garage than you score a new client whose items fill it right back up again. You may be able to store three clients' items easily if they're something small like toys, but one client with something larger, such as bicycles, is another story. It could mean the hassle and expense of renting extra space or otherwise just surrendering your house to the chaos of clutter.

Secondly, you'll be responsible for client items while they're in your care. That means that you'll need to compensate the owner if anything happens to them such as theft, loss, or damage. While it may seem like common sense to be careful with them, accidents happen, and you'll need to be ready for that eventuality.

THE CHALLENGE OF FINDING THE BEST ITEMS TO SELL

This is the biggest consideration and the number one reason people struggle with running a Selling Assistant business. Some find themselves doing too much work for not enough money. Fixing this comes down to one very simple thing: Make sure you're taking on the right items.

Some items have a high work-to-income ratio. In other

words, they may take you hours to list and yield only a small income. The solution to this is to choose your items carefully. The wrong items can mean too much work for what you'll make to sell them.

No matter how carefully you select your items, there will always be at least a few time wasters. Sometimes a client with lots of really high-quality stuff asks you to also sell a couple of low-value items, and you'll do it because you want the big ticket inventory. Sometimes a client misrepresents what they have and you don't realize it until you're already contracted into the job and committed to listing it. Sometimes the market just doesn't perform how you expect it to and you get burned.

The saving grace to this downside is that the reverse is also true. Sometimes an item that takes almost no time to list will yield massive profits, a client's items will actually be better than advertised, or items unexpectedly sell for more than you expect. As long as you're regularly choosing the right kind of items, I believe it all evens out in the end.

YES, IT IS WORTH IT.

If you're getting overwhelmed by my brutal honesty, let me assure you that you'd be far worse off if I were just puffing you up to believe everything was going to be perfect and that you'd be a millionaire by noon. Instead, I'm giving you the truth. Being a Selling Assistant is a job, and like any other job, it has its good parts and bad. But speaking as someone who's done this for two decades, I can assure you that no matter how it looks like the pluses and minuses tally up, the sum is still a fantastic opportunity that is well worth your giving a try. If it wasn't, I sure as heck wouldn't be wasting my time doing it myself and wouldn't bother to encourage others.

YOU CAN DO IT.

I consider Selling Assistance to be a complimentary and not competitive service, which is why I wish you nothing but success with your SA services. The beauty of all the freedom you get in designing a service like this is that your resulting business will be nothing like mine even if we started from the same foundations because you are uniquely you and your business cannot help but be an extension of that. It gives me genuine pleasure to be able to share my knowledge in the hopes that it will help someone like you to be able to enjoy the freedom I've experienced because of my Selling Assistant services. I am forever grateful that I got involved with selling items for others and the flexibility it offers because it enabled me to do things in my life that I never would have been able to do otherwise. And something that good should, nay must, be shared.

My goal with this book was to share what I've learned in my two decades selling things for other people to give you the best possible chance of replicating, and hopefully surpassing, my successes. I could have probably fired you up with false promises of easy work-from-home-in-your-pjs riches, but I wanted to present reality, the good and the bad, to give you an accurate picture of what you were getting into. Only you can tell me if I succeeded, and I hope you will!

If you run into any issues not covered in these pages, spot a mistake or have additional questions, please don't hesitate to contact me. I've already had to rewrite this book completely from scratch three times, making a few small changes or releasing a revision will be nothing compared to that!

Thank you for sticking with me until the end and here's to your future successes.

Now get out there and sell their stuff!

Your Selling Assistant Assistant,

T. W. Seller

ABOUT THE AUTHOR

T. W. Seller started selling online in the mid-90s as a teenager with a dial-up modem. Now more than two decades later, Seller's sold just about everything and sold it just about everywhere. From navigating Amazon's ever-changing e-commerce jungle to earning PowerSeller and Top Rated rankings as an eBay Trading Assistant and high volume seller, T. W. Seller has a wealth of e-commerce knowledge and experience to share about selling almost anything online.

On TheWhineSeller.com, T. W. Seller shares strategies for selling success on topics like publishing, promotion, productivity and other life hacks for today's e-commerce entrepreneur. A regular guest on the original eBay Radio, she was also one of the first Social Media Sellers named by the official eBay Ink Blog for her lively social media presence. As a speaker and author, Seller has connected with sellers and writers from around the world as in expert panels, talks and workshops and through her books about e-commerce and beyond.

T. W. Seller also writes fiction and plays as Hillary DePiano.

For more information about books, articles and more, visit T. W. Seller online at TheWhineSeller.com.

www.ingramcontent.com/pod-product-compliance
Lightning Source LLC
Chambersburg PA
CBHW070723220326
41598CB00024BA/3281